THE BASEBALL CODE

THE BASEBALL CODE

GARY L. WATTS

STUART TARTLY PRESS

This is a work of fiction; the novel's story and characters are fictitious. Any public places, institutions, or historical figures mentioned in the story serve only as a backdrop to the characters and their actions, which are wholly imaginary.

Stuart Tartly Press
17216 Saticoy Street, #226
Lake Balboa, CA. 91406-2103

ISBN: 978-1-953595-21-8 (Hardcover Edition)
ISBN: 978-1-953595-19-5 (Paperback Edition)
ISBN: 978-1-953595-20-1 (eBook Edition)

For Julie, Aaron, and Jacqueline

"Beauty is truth, truth beauty,—that is all
 Ye know on earth, and all ye need to know."

— JOHN KEATS

"Where were you when I laid the foundation of the
 earth? . . .
when the morning stars sang together
 and all the heavenly beings shouted for joy?

— JOB 38:4, 7 (*NRSV*)

CONTENTS

PROLOGUE

Nothing should die in spring—when everything is green and sprouting with new life.

But that is when they put her in the ground. The thick, coiled ropes lowering the casket into the dark earth.

It didn't seem right.

But I didn't know if I believed in right anymore.

PART I

PRACTICE

1

A year later

I was drifting, but the sound was tugging at me. I opened my eyes and blinked to focus on the Renoir print across from me on the wall. The sound again. It was the doorbell. I set my book on the arm of the chair and stood up. My glasses fell out of my lap.

"Crap!"

I bent down to pick them up, feeling the stiffness of my age. The doorbell again.

"Okay. Okay. I'm coming."

I opened the door and looked into the face of a young woman with a grade-school-aged boy beside her. I recognized her. She lived two houses down. We went to the same church, and she had been part of a small group with me for a few weeks when she first moved in a year ago or so.

"Hi. I'm sorry to bother you. But I live just down the street. My name is Ashley. I go to the church. I—"

"Yeah. Hi Ashley; I know who you are."

"Well, I'm really sorry to bother you, but I have a favor to ask. My son missed the bus this morning, and I'm starting a new job today, and I'm already late, and I, well, I was wondering if you would ever be willing to drive him to school —like today? I'm really sorry to ask."

"Sure. No problem. I'd be happy to. Which school is it?"

"It's Lincoln. Oh, thank you so much. Really, you have no idea. I really appreciate it. Noah knows the way too, so he can tell you. Thank you so much, really."

She turned to the boy next to her.

"Noah, you help show Mr. Richards where to go, Okay? And be respectful."

"Okay, Mom."

And she was gone.

Noah was wearing blue jeans and a Jurassic Park T-shirt. I wasn't sure how old he was. It's an ability I've lost with age. All young people just look young. What struck me about Noah was his hair and his eyes.

His hair was thick dark brown, neatly combed with a swath hanging across his forehead at an angle. His eyes were also deep brown with something wistful behind them that I couldn't quite put my finger on.

"Wait over by the driveway, and I'll back the car out."

"Okay."

I closed the front door and went through the kitchen and out the side door into the garage. I hit the button to open the garage and then backed the car out, watching to make sure that Noah wasn't standing in the way. Noah hopped in. We backed out and started down the street.

I didn't need any directions to find Lincoln. It was the closest elementary school in the area. But it was still over a mile away, so there was time to talk, which was a little awkward.

"How old are you, Noah?"

"Ten."

"What grade are you in?"

"Fifth."

I wasn't a great conversationalist. That was Susan's area. I claimed this was because I was too reflective, because I over-thought everything before I said it. Susan said I was just unfriendly. Once I replied that I wasn't half as unfriendly as I pretended not to be. I thought that was witty. Susan said I should have thought *that* over before I said it.

Anyway, Susan would have known what to say to get a ten-year-old giving more than one-word responses. She said that conversation wasn't difficult. It was just about taking an interest in the other person, finding out what he or she delighted in. I was trying to remember what might delight a ten-year-old when Noah's voice caught me by surprise.

"Do you like baseball?"

"What?"

"Do you like baseball? I like baseball. I've got my glove in my backpack."

"Sure. I like baseball. Do you play at school?"

"Sometimes at recess."

"Do you ever play five-hundred?"

"What's that?"

"It's a game where one guy hits the ball. Then whoever catches it gets points. You get more points if you catch a fly ball than if you catch a grounder. Once someone gets five hundred points, he gets to bat."

"Oh, nah. We usually just play catch. But my mom signed me up for Summer League this summer. We play at the park."

"What position do you like?"

"I like second base. But I'm usually in the outfield."

"Outfield is good. It's fun to catch fly balls. I used to like to play center field."

"Yeah, I guess so. No one hits the ball out there much.

7

Sometimes I just sit on the bench and watch. I'm not very good."

"Well, it's just a matter of practice. I loved baseball when I was your age. I played every chance I got. I didn't want to stop to eat. The more I played, the better I got. It's all about practice. Just keep working at it."

"Yeah, I guess so."

We had arrived at Lincoln. I pulled into the driveway area alongside the cement curb for drop-off. Noah opened the door and started to get out.

"Thanks for the ride, Mr. Richards."

"Sure."

Kids were milling around, laughing and talking, bumping into each other. Noah walked up the sidewalk with his head down and disappeared through the glass doors. I eased the car back out of the drive onto the street and headed home. Then I thought maybe I'd drive through McDonald's on the way and get a cup of coffee. But I wasn't sure. I could make the coffee at home just as easily.

But it was something to do.

2

I knew what I was talking about with respect to practice. I won a trophy in the Apalachin Little League for the "Most Improved Player." At the time, I wasn't happy with it. I wanted "Most Home Runs" or "Best Starting Pitcher."

But "Most Improved" has grown on me. The kid with the most home runs probably had a birthday that fell just right so that he was older and bigger than the others. The starting pitcher's dad probably coached the team. But the "most improved" was the one who was dedicated, who worked at it. That was me.

I was eight years old, and I was already crazy about baseball.

Apalachin was a rural town in upstate New York. So the Yankees were my team. It was 1960, and Mickey Mantle was in his prime. He hit 40 home runs that year, including what some claim to be the longest ever—643 feet! The next year, he raced Roger Maris to try to top Ruth's record of 60. Maris hit 61 and Mantle hit 54. Any New York kid had to love the Yankees.

I had a Mickey Mantle baseball card. You got baseball cards by buying a pack of gum that came with a few cards in it. The cards had pictures of players on the front. On the back were stats about the player, like batting average, home runs, and stolen bases. My friends and I collected cards and stored them in old cigar or shoe boxes.

We pulled them out and sorted them over and over, comparing them and arguing about who had the best. We traded them at times. But that was tough because everyone knew that no one was giving up a Roger Maris or a Bobby Richardson—and certainly not a Mickey Mantle.

My friends liked collecting baseball cards, and everyone loved Mickey Mantle. But my enthusiasm for the game was on a whole different level. I bought a large paperback pictorial rule book with a bright red cover. I sat in my room and read through it again and again.

I knew the distance between the bases was 90 feet. I knew from the pitcher's rubber to home plate was 60 feet and 6 inches. I knew that if a pitcher straddled the rubber without the ball in his hand that it was a balk.

I even knew the esoteric infield fly rule, that if a fly ball is hit to the infield with less than two out and two or three runners on base that the batter is immediately called out by the umpire to stop the infielder from purposely dropping the fly to make a double or triple play.

I played baseball every moment that I could. My first new baseball glove was a Rawlings. I still remember the smell of it. It came with a can of Glovolium glove oil. I rubbed some oil into the pocket of the glove. Then every night, I put a ball in the pocket and a rubber band around the glove to hold it tight.

On Saturday morning, I would pick up my glove, take off the rubber band, slip my hand into the well-formed pocket, and head out the back door looking for my friends. Except in the summer when there was Little League, we never had enough kids to have a real game. And we didn't have a field. But

I had a big, open back yard, and if we got at least three kids we could play five-hundred.

Five-hundred worked like this. One kid was the batter. Everyone else was in the field. The batter tossed the ball up in the air and hit it on the way back down. He tried to hit fly balls but frequently hit grounders instead. A grounder caught was worth twenty-five points. A fly ball was one-hundred points. A ball caught on one bounce was seventy-five points and on two bounces was fifty points.

But if you touched the ball and didn't catch it, you lost the same points that you would have got for catching it. So if you dropped a fly ball, you lost one-hundred points, and so on. The first kid to get to five hundred became the next batter.

My mom told us we had to hit the ball away from the house. There were two problems with this. First, there were no fences between yards, nothing to stop the ball. So if we stood by the house and hit the ball toward the back of the yard, when kids missed it, it just kept going, through our back yard and on through the neighbor's back yard. So we all had to wait until one of us chased the ball down and ran back with it before the batter could hit another one.

Second, our house was on the east side of the lot. So in the morning, if we hit from where the house was, the fielders were looking into the sun. This made it hard to catch fly balls. So despite my mom's warnings, we sometimes hit the ball toward the house.

That morning, that's what we were doing. I was batting, and my friends Bobby and Scott were in the field. I tossed the ball up in the air and swung. I topped it. The ball dribbled along the ground and died about twenty feet in front of me. No way was either Bobby or Scott going to run all the way in to pick it up, so I had to trot out, grab it myself, and then run back to home plate.

I tossed it up again. A swing and a complete miss.

"Strike two!" yelled Bobby.

"Okay, here it comes," I said. I tossed, swung again, and hit a grounder that Bobby caught. He threw it back in. The next one was a grounder to Scott that he dropped.

"That's minus twenty-five," I yelled.

The next two or three were also grounders, and Bobby was getting impatient.

"C'mon. Hit one in the air."

"I'm tryin'."

"No you're not. You just wanna stay up."

"Do not! I'm tryin'."

"No you're not!"

"Am so!"

I *was* trying, and I was frustrated. And now I was angry. I tossed the ball up, fixed my eyes on the red seams, and swung my anger out.

Thwack!

The sound was so pure that even if I hadn't seen the ball take off into the sky, I would have known that it was too much. Bobby and Scott didn't even take a step to try to run it down. They just turned around and looked in time to catch the second sound as the ball crashed through the kitchen window.

Everything stood still for one eternal moment. Then it broke into a fury.

Bobby and Scott were off, running as fast as they could, across the yard and down the street into the neighborhood behind our house. I panicked, dropped the bat, and tore off after them—or with them—I didn't really know. Everything was moving so fast. It seemed like the only thing to do.

I was already three blocks away when it hit me. Where was I going? Bobby could run to his house. Scott could run to his house. I was running away from my mine. I stopped and sat down on the curb. I took several deep breaths to fight back my tears. Then I started the long walk back home.

It ended the way I knew it would. Thankfully, no one had been in the kitchen when the ball hit the window. But it was still a mess and cost a lot to fix. It wasn't the smack on the bottom that bothered me. It was losing my bat, ball, and glove for two weeks. But my mom didn't make us stop playing ball in the back yard. She knew how much I loved baseball. And she knew I needed the practice if I wasn't going to get the "Most Improved Player" trophy two years in a row.

3

Susan and I met at our church youth group. I arrived late to a Sunday night meeting and slumped down into a chair at the back of the room. David was up front strumming the guitar. The hippie movement was in full swing, and everyone was singing Christian rock and folk music. I joined in on the familiar tune.

I have decided to follow Jesus.
I have decided to follow Jesus.
I have decided to follow Jesus.
No turning back,
No turning back.

David sat down and Tim Lundgren got up. Ugh. Honestly, no one could stand this guy. The church had hired him from a local seminary to be our youth leader. But we didn't think we needed a youth leader. We had met on our own for a long time and resented giving up our freedom. Besides, Tim was arrogant, overbearing, and not very bright. He was more conservative than most of us and didn't like us to question anything. If you asked a question, he stood there staring at you with his mouth half open, bent slightly forward at the waist, looking like Yogi Bear. Then he responded with some pat answer he had memorized.

Tim had been talking for a while, but I wasn't paying attention because something—or I should say someone—else had caught my attention. There was a girl sitting near the front whom I hadn't seen before. She had soft dark brown hair flowing in waves down over her shoulders. I kept trying to catch her profile when she turned to talk to the person next to her. But I couldn't get a good look.

The meeting closed with prayer. I stood up and walked to the front of the room. Several members of the group, including David and the new girl, were standing in a circle chatting. I was shy by nature and hesitant to insert myself. But I was more comfortable here because I had been attending this church since I was ten years old. It felt like family. Still, I joined the circle without saying anything.

David interrupted the conversation.

"Terry, have you met Susan?"

"No. Hi Susan. I'm Terry."

"Hi."

Not only was she pretty, but she had these youthful freckles across her nose and these sparkling, blue eyes.

David continued, "Susan was sharing something with us about the peace sign that she learned from her previous church, and she has a pamphlet. Go on, Susan."

"Well, it says the peace sign is a broken cross. So it isn't just against the war; it's against the Church."

"What's that about a broken cross?" I asked.

Why was I engaging this? Was it my own awkward attempt to get her attention?

"It's the shape," she said, "the line with the two arms. It's like a cross turned upside down with the sides broken and pointed downward."

I was at the beach quite a bit. So I often saw the peace sign on surf vans, VW buses, and random clothing. It didn't strike me that those folks had anything against the Church.

"Do you think the people using the sign know that?" I asked. "Maybe they just think it means peace, and that's all there is to it."

"I suppose so. I don't know," Susan said.

Why didn't I just keep my mouth shut? Did it really matter? She was just passing on something someone else had told her. Now I had probably embarrassed her.

I'm not sure how that encounter ended, but it wasn't exactly love at first sight, at least not on her part.

Despite getting off on the wrong foot, I knew I wanted to ask Susan out. So when I thought enough time had passed that she might have forgotten about my initial blunder, I decided to call her up and ask her to Disneyland. Disneyland was the perfect place for a date. There were hours and hours of entertaining things to do—rides, stores, food, and shows. If things didn't go well, you could leave whenever you wanted. If things were going great, you could stay till midnight.

I sat with the telephone on my lap, practicing the call in my head.

"Hello. This is Terry. I was wondering if ..."

No. "Wondering" sounds like I'm unsure of myself.

"Hello. This is Terry. Are you free this Saturday?"

But that gives her an immediate out.

"Hello. This is Terry. Would you like to go to Disneyland with me this Saturday?"

Yup. That's the most straightforward. The most confident.

It's not that I hadn't asked anyone out before. But I didn't have a lot of practice. I had spent most of high school studying and playing baseball. I took a deep breath, grabbed the receiver, and began to dial. My heart was starting to pound. It was ringing. The script was playing in my head. I heard someone pick up.

"Hello?" It wasn't Susan's voice. I don't know why, but that threw me.

"Hello, um, is Susan there?" Now I was starting to breathe a little faster.

"May I ask who's calling?"

"It's Terry Richards."

"Just a minute. I'll get her."

I was starting to panic a bit because the script had to change. I couldn't tell her who was calling and then ask her about Saturday because now she already knew who was calling. But I couldn't just start off with "Do you want to go to Disneyland?" That seemed too abrupt. I didn't have time to think it through.

"Hello."

"Hi Susan . . . How are you?"

"I'm fine. How are you?"

"Good. Yeah, um, I was wondering about Saturday, um . . ."

"Oh, yeah, Saturday night. The sport's night at the church. I'm glad you called me. You were on my list. Are you going to be able to come? It starts at 6:30 p.m."

"Um, yeah, sure. Just wanted to let you know."

"Okay. See you there."

"Okay. Bye."

And just like that, Disneyland morphed into sports night in the church parking lot. Don't get me wrong. I loved sports nights—volleyball and basketball. Sports were my thing. But in this case, I'd been hoping for something a little less team oriented.

It turned out okay, however, because at the sports night, I worked up the courage to ask her face to face if she would go to Disneyland with me the next weekend, and she said she would love to.

Disneyland was everything I had hoped for. It was a beautiful, bright sunny day. We walked down Main Street and bought pickles out of a barrel in the Market House old-fashioned grocery. We stopped to watch the horse-drawn streetcar go by as we crossed the roundabout toward Sleeping Beauty's Castle, hustling to make sure we got to the Matterhorn before the line was too long.

We went on every ride we could—the Bobsleds, the Haunted Mansion, the Pirates of the Caribbean, the Jungle Cruise, It's a Small World, the Country Bear Jamboree. We even went on a bunch of smaller rides in Fantasyland. Those little rides were great because we squeezed in together, and when we whipped around a corner, Susan's head would bounce over my shoulder, and her beautiful, long brown hair would brush against my face.

We ate dinner at the Blue Bayou.

The one issue I hadn't thought about was the long waits in line for rides, often half an hour or more. This meant having to be good at conversation, which didn't come naturally to me. But Susan was so good at this that it wasn't a problem. She was completely relaxed about it. She laughed, asked questions about me, talked about herself, and brought up topics we both had interest in. We were standing in line for the Matterhorn when Susan asked,

"How do you think our bible studies have been going lately?"

"What do you mean?"

"I mean since Tim started leading them."

"Oh, yeah. Well, he sure doesn't like anyone to ask questions."

"No kidding, right? What was that lecture about rock music all about—the evil beat, two shorts and a long, and all that stuff?"

"I don't know. He sure didn't want to hear what any of us thought about it."

"What *do* you think?" she asked.

"About what? About rock music?"

"Yeah."

"Well, I think it's just music. Some of it's good. Some of it's not. Like most things, I don't think you can make a single judgment about all of it."

"Me too," she said, "but not Tim. I'm pretty sure he believes it's some kind of communist plot."

We both started laughing. When Susan laughed, she had this way of rocking her head and shoulders slightly backwards and then in a circular motion. It was delightful.

"I asked him," she added, "if he thought girls should still cover their heads because Paul says that to the Corinthians, and he said 'Yes.' I think if Tim ever comes over to my house, I'll answer the door with a paper bag over my head."

Her head started to rock back, and we both broke out laughing again. I just wanted to hug her. She was so amazing. As the sun went down, we started running around, hand in hand, trying to get to as many rides as possible to use up the rest of our ticket books. Then we sat on the Mark Twain Riverboat in the warm darkness and ate ice cream.

We left at midnight.

It was late when we got back to her house. I walked up to the door with her and told her what a wonderful time I had. She said the same. I was just ready to turn away when she leaned toward me.

It's impossible to describe a first kiss. I'm sure someone has tried. But words won't bear the weight. There is one thing I can say for certain, however.

It doesn't require any practice.

PART II

WARM-UP

4

Catch is a kind of conversation. You throw the ball, and the other person throws it back. It's give and take. There's a rhythm to it. If you don't hold up your end because you drop the ball too often or you can't throw it all the way back, the conversation falters. Some catch conversations are livelier than others. You can fling one side-arm, toss in a grounder or a pop-up, or do a Willie Mays basket catch. It's all about anticipating what your partner finds engaging.

But catch also includes regular conversation. While you throw the ball back and forth, you talk. It might be about baseball. It might be about anything. Whether it's warming up before a game or a casual diversion after dinner, there is rarely a silent game of catch. There's something about the one kind of conversation that encourages the other.

My dad and I didn't talk a lot. He was quiet and so was I. But our best conversations were when we were playing catch. I'd grab our gloves after dinner and ask him if he wanted to play some catch. Looking back, I'm sure he was tired after a day's work and after fighting the L.A. freeways. But he usually said yes. I'd toss him the catcher's mitt and run to the other side of the yard.

"Here comes my fast ball." Pop! The ball hit his glove.

"Hey, slow it down there! What have I told you about warming up?"

My dad was big on warming up your arm. He hurt his arm when he was young trying to throw curve balls, and now he was cautious. I knew better, but I liked to throw it fast.

"Reach up for the sky," he said, "then out in front, then to the side. Really stretch. Now again. Okay. Now let's just toss it easy for a while."

We threw the ball back and forth, getting a little faster each time. Then my dad asked,

"How's Little League practice going?"

"Pretty good, I guess."

"What does that mean?"

"Coach has me playing center field. But I'd rather be at second base."

"Are there other kids who like to play second?"

"Yeah. But I'm as good as any of them, maybe better; it doesn't seem fair."

I threw the ball with a little extra steam, and it snapped into Dad's mitt.

"How are you at center field?" he asked as he tossed it back.

"I can run fast, so I catch most of the fly balls."

Dad stepped quickly to his left and stretched his arm out to snag my throw.

"Whoa, that one almost got away. You know, something like that happened to me too."

"What do you mean?"

"When I was in high school, I was big for my age. So the coach wanted me to play catcher because I could block the plate. It wasn't my favorite position, but that's the way it was."

"That doesn't seem fair either."

Dad caught the ball and then paused for a moment before throwing it back.

"Did you ever hear of Johnny Klippstein?"

"Nope."

He threw one on the ground that I had to bend down and watch into my glove.

"He was a pitcher for Cincinnati back in 1956, while we still lived in New York. He was pitching a game against Milwaukee, and he was having a good night. He was a little wild but otherwise throwing strong.

"In the second inning, he walked a couple and hit a batter, and Milwaukee wound up scoring a run on a sacrifice fly. So Milwaukee was ahead one to nothing. But even though his team was behind, after seven innings, Klippstein still had a no-hitter going."

"Wow, did he make it?"

"Well, you have to listen to the rest of the story."

He tossed one up in the air so that I had to move back a few steps and wait for it to come down.

"He had the no-hitter going through seven innings. But they were still losing one to nothing. In the top of the eighth, Cincinnati got a man on second and Klippstein was up to bat. The manager pulled him and put in a pinch hitter."

"Are you kidding? Why? Why would he do that?"

"Because they were a run behind and had a man in scoring position. Klippstein wasn't a great hitter, so a pinch hitter had a better chance of scoring the runner, tying up the game, and giving them a chance to win."

"But he had a no-hitter goin'. That wasn't fair."

"I guess it depends on what you mean by 'fair.' If you mean what was good for Klippstein as an individual player, then sure, a no-hitter would have been good. But if you mean what was good for the team, then winning the game was good because the point isn't to get no-hitters. The point is to win games. So it depends on whether fair means what's good for one person or what's good for everyone."

I rolled the ball around in my bare hand, looking at the seams. Then I just held onto it for the moment.

"So you're saying I should play center field."

"No. Not exactly. There's nothing wrong with you telling your coach what you want to do and asking him why he won't let you play second base, I mean, if you want to. But the point is that maybe he put you in center field because there are other kids who can do a good job playing second base but no one else who can play center field as well as you. You like chasing flies, right?"

"Yeah."

"So if it turns out the coach has you there for the good of the team, it's probably best not to worry about a different position and to just enjoy chasing down the fly balls."

5

The engine started to bog down. The mower was showing its age, just like me. I pushed down on the handle and rocked it back on its rear wheels to take some pressure off the blades. But it backfired and died anyway. This was the third time, and it was beginning to get annoying. I put my left hand on the handle and pulled the starter cord as hard as I could. Nothing. A second time. It started to chug for a moment, but then nothing again. A third time. It sputtered slowly and then took off.

I continued pushing it down the front lawn. There had to be something wrong with the carburetor. It ran fine after it got warmed-up, but it was taking longer and longer every time. I was going to have to take it in and have someone look at it. Maybe I should just buy a new one.

Something flashed by my left side. I flinched and turned in time to see a baseball bounce and roll into the bushes by the front of the house.

"Sorry, Mr. Richards." The voice was followed by running footsteps. I recognized the dark brown hair falling across the forehead.

"Hey, Noah. No problem. Just don't hit me on the head."

He pulled the ball from under a branch, turned and scurried back the way he'd come, yelling over his shoulder,

"Okay, Mr. Richards. Sorry."

When the ball went by, I'd let go of the safety bar and the engine stopped. So I had to start the mower again. My arm was getting tired. Thankfully, it started on the first pull. I only had a couple more passes to finish up. I had turned and was pushing back in the direction the ball had come from when I saw it come bouncing through the neighbor's yard and roll to a stop a few feet to my right. I wasn't about to start the mower again. So this time, I kept pushing. Noah was just a few seconds behind. He grabbed the ball.

"Sorry."

"Don't worry about it."

He took off, and I turned and made my last pass along the sidewalk. I dropped the safety bar, turning off the mower. Then I pushed it up the driveway and into the garage. As I walked back out of the garage to grab the rake I'd left leaning up against the wall, the ball came bouncing into the yard again. This was a little much; I was familiar with awkward attempts to grab someone's attention.

I walked over and picked up the ball. Noah wasn't far behind. I held onto the ball.

"Hey, Noah, are you havin' a game with someone?"

"No. It's just me. I'm hittin' it with my bat. It's kind of a toy bat, but it works okay."

I tossed the ball up and down in my hand and hung on to it.

"Do you have a minute?"

"I guess so."

"Have a seat on the porch. I'll be right back."

I handed Noah the ball, opened the front door, and went into the house. I walked into the kitchen and opened the refrigerator. Then I took two ice cream bars out of the freezer, walked back outside, and sat down by Noah.

"You like ice cream?" I handed him one of the bars.

"Sure."

We both unwrapped the bars and starting eating. I was stuck as usual, trying to think of how to engage a ten-year-old. Why was it so hard? I took another couple of bites.

"How's school goin'?"

"Okay, I guess."

Another couple bites of ice cream. "Do you have a favorite class?"

"Not really."

"Hey, looks like you got some chocolate on your chin."

"Oh?" He wiped his hand across the bottom of his face.

This wasn't working. Susan would already be laughing and teasing, and Noah would be telling her his life story. I looked down at the steps and noticed the ball lying at Noah's feet.

Of course.

"Hey," I said, "wanna play some catch?"

"Yeah, sure! I'll go get my mitt. Be right back."

"Okay."

I walked into the garage to look for my mitt. I hadn't touched it in years, but I thought I knew where it was. I pulled a cardboard box off the shelf above my head on the side of the wall. It felt a little too heavy. I set it on the floor and opened it—books. I lifted it back up to the shelf.

I stood there for a minute thinking. After Susan's funeral, I went on a cleaning spree and took a bunch of my old stuff to the Goodwill. But there's no way I would have ever given away my glove. Wait a minute. I walked over to a round, white plastic trash can that was under the work bench.

I took off the lid. There were several aluminum bats. I pushed them aside. Near the bottom of the can was the glove. I reached in and pulled it up. It still had string tied around it and a ball in the pocket. The rawhide lacing tying the fingers together was broken in one place. I'd have to fix that later.

"Mr. Richards?"

Noah had returned with his ball and glove and was peeking timidly into the garage.

"Right here," I said, walking out of the garage onto the driveway. I motioned to Noah to go down to the other side of the yard.

"Let's warm up our arms."

Noah threw me the ball. I caught it and threw it back to him. It glanced off his glove, bounced against his chest, and fell to the ground in front of him. I hadn't thrown it hard, so he wasn't hurt.

"Sorry."

"Don't worry about it. We're just having fun. Keep your eyes on the ball and watch it all the way into your glove."

I caught it and threw it back to him again. This time he caught it.

"Good catch!"

Noah tossed the ball back to me, but it was way to my right. I jumped fast and backhanded it.

"Wow! Good catch, too, Mr. Richards."

"Thanks. So you say school is goin' okay?"

"Well, not really, I don't like it that much."

"What don't you like?"

My throw bounced off the tip of Noah's glove and rolled behind him. He ran back and picked it up.

"I don't like math."

He threw the ball back, and it bounced once on the ground before reaching me.

"Why don't you like it?"

"It's kinda hard. We're doin' fractions, and I don't always understand how they work."

"Yeah. Fractions can be hard. Did you know that I was a math teacher?"

"Really?"

"Yup."

"Yuck!"

I broke out laughing. I had started to throw the ball back, but I had to stop. When Noah saw me, he started laughing too.

"Sorry, Mr. Richards, I guess."

"That's okay." I was still chuckling. "Lots of kids don't like math. Sometimes you need someone to show you how it works. Does your mom or dad help you?"

"Nah. My dad moved to New York after Christmas, and my mom is pretty busy."

I knew Noah's parents were divorced. When Ashley was in the small group with me, she was alone. But I had seen Frank around from time to time in the past, and I didn't know he had moved.

"Maybe I can help you with your math homework sometime."

"Yeah. I don't know. I don't really like to do it. I'd rather play baseball."

"I suppose. But you know, math is just like baseball. It's all about practice. The more you practice the better you are at it, and the easier it gets.

"So get ready. I'm going to throw you some grounders. Get your feet apart. Bend your knees. Get on your toes and get your glove out in front of you. Are you ready?"

"Yup."

I threw a grounder right at him. He lowered his glove and stopped it, but it rolled back out.

"Watch it all the way in," I said.

I threw another one the same way. This time he got it. Next,

I threw one a little to his left. He got that one too. Then to the right. That one got by.

"That side is harder," Noah said.

"Yup. That's because you have to reach your glove across your body and catch it backhand. But you'll get it. We'll keep workin' at it."

I threw Noah a bunch more grounders, some to the right, some to the left. Then I held the ball in my hand and walked it back to him.

"Okay. That's it for today. I'm an old guy. I've gotta rest."

"Where did you learn about baseball, Mr. Richards?"

"I used to play with my dad, just like we were playing today. He taught me a lot."

Noah looked up at me from under the swath of brown hair falling across his forehead.

"I miss my dad," he said.

"I know what you mean. I miss mine too."

6

After Disneyland, Susan and I went to dinner a couple of times. We also saw each other at church and often sat together. So after a Wednesday night prayer meeting, I asked her if she'd like to go to the beach on Saturday, and she said, "Sure."

I loved the beach—surfing and body surfing, sitting in the sun and watching the breakers crash against the shore, feeling the wet, cool sand against your feet as you walked along next to the water. Nothing better.

I picked her up around 9:00 a.m. We jumped in my VW Bug and took off. We were headed to Zuma, a beach a little north of Malibu. To get there, after driving the freeway for a bit, you take Malibu Canyon.

Malibu Canyon is iconic. It winds its way up over the coastal mountains and down to the Pacific Coast Highway. It has a peculiar beauty. In the middle of summer, the hills, brown with dry chaparral and dotted with oak and sycamore, stand out against the crisp blue sky.

We pulled into the parking lot, right up against the cinderblock wall that separated the asphalt from the sand of the beach. I threw my wallet in the glove compartment, and

Susan shoved her purse under the seat. Then we pulled out the cooler, locked the car, each grabbed a handle, and started off toward the water. Since we both wanted to swim, we found a spot close to the water to lay out our towels. We set the cooler down and walked toward the surf.

Whenever a wave retreated from the shore, we could see the sand crabs burrowing quickly into the sand. The froth washed over our feet. The water at Zuma never gets much higher than 65 degrees even in the middle of summer. So it's cold when you first get in. We were moving slowly—feet, ankles, knees—until Susan reached down and splashed me with a handful. I had to return the favor. Then it was no holds barred, splashing and kicking water, pushing, and we were in.

The surf wasn't big that day, one to two feet. So we didn't worry about the waves crashing on us. We dove under the breaks and floated over the swells. We caught a few short rides across the faces. When we started to get cold, we got out, sat on our towels, and put some sun-tan lotion on each other's backs.

"Want a Coke?" I asked.

"Sure."

I opened the cooler and pulled out a Coke for each of us and a package of Red Vines. I handed her a Coke and offered her some of the licorice. She declined. I stuck a piece between my teeth and threw the bag on the towel.

One of the things I loved about Susan was the way she conversed. It was like a good game of catch—easy and relaxed. She tossed interesting questions or thoughtful comments my way and fielded my replies with effortless precision. But today she hit me with a curve ball on the first throw.

"What do you think love is?"

I had to stall for time. "What?"

"What do you think love is? Is it a feeling or is it an action?"

I still wasn't ready, and talking about love with a girl I really liked was making me a little nervous. I had to throw it back again.

"I guess I'd have to think about it a little. What do you think?"

"I was thinking about Jesus saying that we should love our neighbors as ourselves. I mean, that's like a commandment, right?"

"Yeah."

"But you can't be commanded to *feel* a certain way. You can be commanded to *act* a certain way. That makes it seem like love is an action."

Okay—putting the subject in a religious and philosophical context made me relax a little. I tossed back a reply.

"That makes sense. I suppose that's how we can 'love our enemies.' You don't have to have warm feelings about them. You just have to treat them better than they treat you."

Susan had been leaning on one elbow. She sat up and pulled up her knees. When she was out in the sun, the freckles across her nose stood out.

"But do you think you can treat someone well if you continue to have bad feelings toward them?" she asked.

"That's a good question. It seems like sooner or later your bad feelings might push you to do something bad."

"And maybe treating someone well often enough will make you start to have better feelings about them," Susan responded.

Then she paused in thought for a moment. It was as if she were tossing the ball up and down in her hand before throwing it back. Then she added,

"You know, my parents are divorced, and—"

I did know that Susan's parents were divorced, not because she had told me, but because David from church had told me. It was a small, conservative church and things like that got around. Susan continued,

"I think about what happened sometimes. I mean, when

they were first married, they loved each other, you know, with feelings and actions. Somewhere that changed. What happened first? Did their feelings change? Or did they stop treating each other with love? Maybe when they started having problems, if they had started *acting* more lovingly, they would have recovered their feelings."

I didn't know how to respond. Not only was the conversation about love moving into the area of romance, which made me nervous again, but Susan was talking about her parents, and it didn't seem to me that I was in a position to have an opinion about something so personal.

"I don't know. Maybe romantic love is something different."

"Maybe. But it involves feelings and action just like loving your neighbor. And if the way you act can change the way you feel, then maybe it's not so different. Maybe it's all about what we *choose* to do and what we *choose* to feel."

"So would that mean that we could choose to love anyone, in a romantic sense?"

"I don't know," Susan said, "but it does seem like love might be more under our control than we usually think it is."

It was my turn to hold the ball in my hand and ponder for a while. I looked at Susan. The sun was glancing off her face. I loved being around her. She looked up and caught my eyes. I smiled at her and turned to look out at the ocean.

"Hey," Susan's voice broke in, "I'm gonna go in for another swim. Wanna come?"

"No. I think I'll read for a little."

I picked up the copy of *The Sun Also Rises* that I was reading for a lit class I had as a general education requirement. I never did like Hemingway. Fitzgerald and even Faulkner were more to my taste.

I started reading. The sun was beating down. It was getting pretty hot. I don't know how long I'd been at it when I decided that I might jump in after all. I set the book down, stood up, and looked out at the water to find Susan.

She wasn't right in front of me. I looked down the beach to the right. Then I saw her. She was out about even with the breakers but in an area where no waves were breaking and where there were patches of foam here and there around her. She was swimming toward the shore but not making any progress. I knew immediately what the problem was.

I ran down along the shore until I was even with Susan. Then I dove into the water and started swimming out toward her. When I got close enough that she could see me, I motioned to her to follow me, and I started swimming parallel to the shore.

I watched so I could see she was doing the same. After about twenty yards, I could feel that we were out of the rip current. I swam the rest of the way out and took one of her arms. She was a little out of breath.

"You're fine now. We'll just head to shore, and let the waves take us in," which is what we did. When the last wave broke and pushed us in, we stood up and walked onto the beach.

"Phew," Susan said, "I'm lucky you were there. I was getting tired. I'm not sure what would have happened if you hadn't seen me."

"Well, I'm glad I saw you too. But you weren't very far out. The waves are small today, and the rip wasn't very strong. If you had gotten much further out, the lifeguard would have seen you and gone out after you with his rescue can."

We walked up a little further onto the beach. Then Susan, turned, threw her arms around me and hugged me tight.

"You're pretty cold," I said. "We should get back to the towels so you can dry off and let the sun warm you up."

But what I thought was,

"She can do that for as long as she likes."

As I was driving home after dropping Susan off, my thoughts floated back to our conversation about the nature of love. It made sense that love was an action that could affect our feelings. We made choices about everything in life, so why shouldn't we make choices about love as well? But despite how much sense all of that made, I couldn't shake the feeling that I was falling pretty hard for Susan and that I wasn't sure there was anything I could do about it.

PART III

THE BASEBALL CODE

7

Dad didn't come to the game. He was working late on a project. I was glad because the game was making me mad.

I had made the majors this year. Our Little League was divided into majors and minors. Once you were old enough to play in the majors, you went to try-outs. The coaches for the different teams watched you at try-outs and then picked players. If you didn't get picked, you might have to play another year in the minors. The teams were named after professional teams. I got picked by the Yankees. That was okay by me because I used to live in New York, and I still liked players like Mickey Mantle and Bobby Richardson.

Our fields were really nice. They had pitching mounds and grass outfields and infields with smooth dirt base paths. There were dugouts and outfield fences with colorful signs on them and stands for the parents. But there were no lights. So the rule was that games had to be finished twenty minutes after the sun went down.

That night, we were playing the Tigers. I was in center field, and I was having a good game. I caught some fly balls. I also got two hits. That wasn't the problem. The problem was that the game was close through the first four innings. It was all tied up at four runs apiece. But we were up in the top of the fifth, and we started hitting everything. We scored five runs, so we were way ahead and there was still nobody out.

The game was running long, and it was getting close to sunset. For any game to be official, at least five innings had to be completed. So for the game to count, the Tigers had to get us out, and then we had to get them out, all before twenty minutes after the sun went down.

That's when it happened.

The Tiger's coach called "time-out." Then he went out to the mound to talk to his pitcher. When the pitcher started throwing again, he just started throwing balls, nowhere near the strike zone. He walked the first batter. Then the second. What was going on? The parents in the stands behind our dugout began booing.

"C'mon, play the game," someone yelled.

Then it hit us. He wasn't *trying* to get us out. He was just going to keep walking batters until the sun went down so the game wouldn't count. We all started yelling,

"Hey, that's not fair!"

"You're tryin' to cheat!"

Our coach was angry too. So he told Billy, the kid who was up, to swing at anything, no matter where it was. The pitcher threw the next one in the dirt about three feet in front of the plate, but Billy swung at it anyway. Now the crowd on both sides was worked up. Everyone was yelling.

The umpire stopped play and walked out to the mound. We couldn't hear what he was saying, but he was waving his arms around and shaking his finger. It was clear that he was telling the pitcher to stop throwing wild and pitch like he was supposed to. He turned and stomped back to his place behind the plate. Billy stepped into the batter's box. The pitcher wound up and threw the next pitch—not only over Billy's head and over the umpire's head but so high that it went over the back-stop and out of the field.

The umpire immediately threw off his mask and called the game.

But that made all of us even more mad because it gave the other coach exactly what he wanted. If the ump called the game before five innings were over, then it didn't count! We were five runs ahead, and now we wouldn't win. All of us were throwing our gloves down and yelling about how unfair it was. But our coach told us that we needed to settle down and go home.

Behind the field was a little two story building. The first floor stored the equipment for taking care of the fields, mowers for the grass and the screen drag for the infield. On the outside, stairs led up to a second story room where the umpires dressed and kept their equipment and records.

When I walked off the field to find my mom, a crowd of parents were still yelling at the ump. I stood and watched. He was backed up against the stairs of the little building. He kept trying to talk but no one was listening. Finally, he turned, ran up the stairs, opened the door, and shut himself in the umpire's room. I heard my mom's voice behind me.

"Hey, Terry, let's go."

"Wow. They're pretty mad. He may have to stay up there all night!"

"Well, we're not staying all night; we've got to get home for dinner. It's a little silly. After all, it's just a game."

"Not really. At least not a fair one."

When my dad got home, I was already in bed and asleep. So I didn't see him until the next day. After dinner, I asked if he would play some catch. He said yes, and we went out into the back yard. We warmed up like usual. Then he threw me a pop-up. I wrapped my arm around behind my back, turned slightly toward the ball, and caught it on the other side of my body.

"That's pretty fancy. Where d'ya learn that?"

"Oh, Greg and I have just been practicing and foolin' around."

"Well, that's good coordination. But don't try it in a game."

"I know."

He threw me another pop-up which I caught normally.

"Your mom tells me your game yesterday was kinda crazy."

"It sure was. The other team cheated us."

"Well, probably not the whole team."

My next throw was off target. It bounced on the ground to my dad's right and rolled behind him.

"I'll get it," I ran past him, picked up the ball, and tossed it to him on my way back.

"Yeah, I guess it was just the pitcher," I said. "He tried to walk everyone so the game wouldn't get over. Why would he do that? It wasn't fair."

"Your mom said it looked like his coach told him to."

"I guess. But it still wasn't fair."

I let a zinger fly that popped into my dad's glove.

"No, it wasn't. You're right about that. But it's hard when you're a kid and your coach tells you to do something. The problem is that the coach shouldn't have told him to do it."

"Yeah, the coach is a dad. Don't dads know what's fair?"

"I don't know. Maybe some do; maybe some don't."

I caught the ball, took it out of my glove, and held it for a few moments in my right hand. I felt the tight red seams press into my fingers.

"Are you thinking about thowin' it back?" Dad asked.

"Sure." I tossed it back. "Well, if some dads don't, I mean, well, so how does anyone know what's fair?"

"That's a tough question. But I think usually someone teaches us, like our parents or friends."

"You mean like school?"

"It could be like that."

He threw a grounder to my left. I shuffled a couple of steps over with ease and watched it into my mitt.

"Nice catch," Dad said, "It could be like school, but it might also be different. Remember the other day when it was really hot, and Mark invited you to go swimming in his pool?"

"Yeah."

"And what did your mother say?"

"She said I couldn't go."

"Why?"

"Because my brother was standing right there, and Mark didn't invite him. He just said, 'Who are you lookin' at? Are you lookin' for an invitation?'"

"Yeah, that's what happened. But what did your mom say was wrong with that?"

"She said it wasn't fair because Ben gets just as hot as Mark or me, and Mark was just being mean. So if Ben couldn't go, then neither could I."

"That's right. She said it wasn't fair, and she explained why. So it wasn't like school, but she was teaching you something."

I threw another fast one that snapped into my dad's mitt.

"Boy, I'm glad I'm wearing the catcher's mitt. You're throwin' some heat today."

"So you think no one ever taught their coach what was fair?" I asked.

"Well, maybe, but it isn't always about knowing what's fair."

"What do you mean?"

Dad bent down and caught one that I bounced on the ground. He kept the ball and took off his mitt.

"Phew," he said, "I think I've had enough. My arm's gettin' tired. Let's sit down for a minute."

We walked over and sat down on the bench of the picnic table on the patio.

"Sometimes," he said, "people know what's fair but just don't want to do it. It's like when your mom told you that you couldn't go swimming if Mark didn't invite your brother too. What if she hadn't been there to say something? Would you have gone when Mark asked you, and left your brother at home?"

"I dunno. Maybe. It was pretty hot."

"That's what I mean. Even without your mom saying something, you probably already knew that wasn't quite fair. But you wanted to go swimming. So you might have gone anyway. So maybe the coach knew that it wasn't fair. But he didn't want to lose the game, so he did it anyway. Even when we know what's right, we still have to choose to do it."

"What makes us do that, I mean, choose the right thing?"

"I'm not sure. Maybe practice, maybe habit, or maybe something else inside us that pushes us to do it. Some people call it having honor or living by a code."

"A code? You mean like Morse Code?"

My dad was an amateur radio operator. He had gotten me interested in studying for a Novice license. To get it, I had to be able to send and receive Morse Code at five words per minute.

My dad chuckled. "No, not like Morse Code. To live by a code means really trying to do what's right."

"So is it called a code because it's like a secret code, something hidden inside you?"

My dad smiled again.

"No, not really. But it is hidden in one sense—that is, you follow your code even when no one is looking. It's like, well, let's see, you know I play golf, right?"

"Yeah."

"Well, after you hit the ball, and then you find it, you're not supposed to move it again before you take your next hit. But maybe the ball landed behind a tree, and if you moved it just a couple of feet you'd have a clearer shot to the green.

"The friend you're playing with is off looking for his ball, so he'd never know. You're all alone, so what do you do? Anyone would be tempted to kick the ball a few feet over. But if you're playing with honor and following a code, then you hit it where it lies."

"I get it. It's kinda like when we're playing five-hundred, and someone hits a fly that you run after, and you try to catch it real close to the ground, but it hits the ground just before it rolls into your mitt, and you swing your mitt up into the air and yell 'I got it' so you can get the hundred points. But you know you really should only get fifty. I've done that."

"Yep, and I've moved my golf ball to a better spot."

"REALLY?" My mouth fell open.

"Sure. Living by a code isn't about being perfect. It's about learning from our mistakes and trying to do better."

"I don't think that coach learned anything from his mistake."

"Well, I don't know. But you learned something from it. And maybe some of the kids on his team did too. But you know, having honor and living by a code isn't just about playing fair in games like baseball and golf. It's about being fair in everything you do."

"So it's about always being fair."

"That's part of it. But it's more than that. It includes other things like telling the truth, helping others, working hard, and doing your best."

I thought about it for a couple moments. Then I looked up at my dad.

"Do you think I have honor?"

He smiled at me.

"I do."

8

I sometimes hopped in the car and drove to Jake's Grocery when I just needed a few items. Jake's was about a mile from the house. It wasn't a discount store like Walmart. It was a locally run business. So the prices weren't low. But it was close, easy, and not crowded. The people there were friendly and remembered my name. I grabbed a cart from the lineup outside and started for the door, but one of the front wheels was frozen. I pushed it up against the wall and grabbed another. I rolled it in and headed up the first aisle.

I've always liked grocery stores. I'm not sure why. Even in high school and college, my friends and I would wander through them, looking at all the tasty stuff we could buy to snack on—shrimp cocktails in little glass bottles, Hostess Fruit Pies, potato chips with sour cream dip, or the bakery section with its endless variety of donuts, muffins, and bagels.

But it wasn't just the food. Late at night, when the stores were almost empty, we would walk through the wide, brightly lit aisles at our leisure with no one paying any attention to us. There was something strangely comforting about it.

But not anymore. Now they reminded me of Susan. To be

fair, almost anything did. It had been more than a year now, but the smallest familiar sight or smell triggered memories that drew me into myself. I used to tease Susan that she could never go into a supermarket and just get the couple of things she had gone in for.

Every aisle or display caught her attention, and before she got out she would have a cartful. If we were in a hurry, I would say, "You just stay in the car, and I'll run it and get the stuff." She would ask why, and I would reply that we didn't have time for a full shopping spree. And then she would tell me that I just had no imagination. Then—

"Hello Terry."

The words yanked me out of my daydream. I realized I had been rolling my cart on autopilot down the cereal aisle. I looked up quickly to my left.

"Oh, sorry. . . . Hi Ashley. How are you?"

"Fine, really. Just grabbing a few things for dinner on my way home from work."

"Oh, yeah, the new job. How's that going?"

"I'm still learning the ropes. But it's okay. By the way, thanks again for taking Noah to school the other day. I really appreciated that—last minute and all, really."

"Any time. It was easy to do. He's a good kid."

"Oh, and thanks for playing ball with him. He loved that— couldn't quit talking about it. He said you were teaching him stuff about baseball. He really loved it."

"Well, to be honest, it's kind of fun for me, too. I loved playing when I was his age. So it gave me a chance to throw the ball around again. I enjoyed it. He said he's gonna play in a Summer League or something."

"Yeah, his father signed him up for that last year. I don't know a lot about it. They play at the park on Saturdays. I hate to admit it, really, but I used it as kind of a bribe to get him to work harder on his schoolwork. I told him if he did better, I'd sign him up again this year. He said he would, but he really hasn't. But I didn't have the heart not to sign him up. He loves baseball so much. So I signed him up anyway."

"He did say something about struggling a little with math."

"Really, ugh, I just don't know what that's about. I can't get him to even try to do his homework."

"I don't know if you knew, but I was a math teacher. I told Noah that I would be willing to help him if he wanted."

"Oh, that is so kind of you, really. But I bet he didn't jump at the offer did he?"

I chuckled.

"Nope. I think he was just amazed that anyone would admit to being a math teacher."

We both laughed.

"Yeah, really, that's the problem. I'm no math teacher, but I can do enough fifth grade math to help. He just has no interest."

"Well, please let him know I'm willing to help him if he would like. Maybe if we play some more ball sometime, we'll have time to talk about it."

Ashley nodded. "Okay, I'll let him know. . . . so . . . yeah."

"Well, have a good evening."

"You too."

I slowly pushed my cart along in the other direction from Ashley, trying to remember what I was doing in the cereal aisle. I didn't usually buy cereal—at least not at Jake's. Then I remembered I had been daydreaming. I didn't mean to be in the cereal aisle at all.

I moved on and picked up some milk, grapes, and peaches. I was almost at the checkout when I paused for a moment. I backtracked and grabbed a box of ice-cream bars, just in case Noah dropped by to play some catch.

~

The rose garden had been Susan's idea. That's why I kept it up so meticulously. It's not that I didn't like roses. I did. But Susan was passionate about them. She not only loved the way they looked, she loved the way they smelled. She would bend down and bury her nose in the petals as if to breathe in the bloom entire. "Ohhhhhh," she would say, "Come here and smell this."

I would. And it smelled good. But I could never get the same enthusiasm. There was a fine tuning in her sense of smell that was beyond my reach. At first, we went to the park a couple of times a week to look at the roses. But she wanted something closer, something she could see and smell every day, something that she could be part of. So we dug up a patch of lawn about ten by twelve in the back yard. I set a brick border around it about a foot high. Then we filled it with topsoil and organic matter, and mulched with bark chippings.

We planted the first rose together, near the center of the garden. I dug the hole, and Susan gently set it in place, pushing the soil in around the roots with her fingers. I don't remember the variety or the name. But it had deep red blooms, and we pronounced the garden an immediate success.

That first rose, however, wasn't doing as well anymore. It probably needed to be replaced. But I couldn't bring myself to do it. Anyway, we had planted about a dozen others around it, so there were plenty of beautiful blooms.

The garden reminds me of Susan. So it's beautiful but also painful. I had just fed the plants and was digging a hole for a new yellow rose in the south corner of the bed nearest the house. But when I set the shovel aside and looked down into the ground, instead of twisted and dangling roots, I saw the thick coiled ropes lowering her casket into the dark earth.

I was frozen.

I don't know how long I had been standing there, gazing

into the hole, transported by that vision, when I heard Noah's voice behind me.

"Hi Mr. Richards."

I turned around.

"Oh . . . Hi Noah."

Over the last couple of weeks, I had been getting to know Noah a little better. He had dropped by two or three times each week after school to play catch. We sometimes played in the backyard, so it wasn't surprising that he looked to find me there. One thing I had learned about Noah was that the wistful something behind his dark brown eyes that I had noticed the first day I met him veiled an uncanny insight a bit beyond his years.

"Were you talkin' to the roses, Mr. Richards?"

"Huh? What?"

"It looked like you were talkin' to the roses. I mean, not out loud, but kinda to yourself. I do that sometimes in school when I'm thinking about baseball, especially in math class."

"Oh, yeah, maybe. You know, you don't have to call me Mr. Richards all the time."

"Oh, sorry. My mom says I can't call adults by their first names. It's disrespectful."

"Well, you do need to pay attention to your mom. Maybe we can figure something else out. Hey, can you help me with something?"

"Sure."

"See that rose over there?" I pointed to the yellow rose that was setting on the ground outside the bed.

"Yeah."

"Pick it up and bring it over here. But be careful. Just grab the plastic can around the bottom. Don't touch the plant itself, and watch out for the thorns."

Noah picked up the rose and carried it over to me. I took the pruning shears, cut the sides of the plastic can, and pulled it away from the plant.

"Okay. Now, I'm going to hold the rose right in the center of the hole I dug. And I want you to push the dirt that's mounded up around the hole down in around the roots. Okay?"

"Okay."

I lifted the rose and set it in the center of the hole. Noah began to shove the dirt down into the sides of the hole.

"Slow down!" I said, "Push it in gently. You don't want to harm the roots."

"Okay." Noah pulled his hands back and then started to push the dirt around the plant slowly and carefully.

"That's it," I said.

When he was done, I smoothed the dirt out around the top. We both stood up.

"How about that. We've planted a rose," I said.

"Yeah. That's pretty cool."

I few minutes later we were playing catch in the backyard. We had warmed up our arms, and I was throwing Noah some grounders to help him practice. One went right under his mitt. He turned and chased it down, ran back to his spot, and threw it back to me.

"Remember, you've got to keep low and watch the ball into your mitt."

"Yeah, I know. I'm not very good at grounders."

"You're fine. It's just a matter of practice. You're getting better each time we play."

"But I still miss a lot."

"It's not how many you miss. It's how many you catch, and you're catching more every day. So just keep focusing on what we talked about. Bend your knees, stay low, eyes on the ball."

"Okay."

I threw one on the ground pretty far to his right. He took a couple of quick steps and put his glove down backhand. The ball hit the glove and bounced back out a few inches in front of him.

"Good stop!" I yelled.

"But I didn't catch it."

"Doesn't matter. It was in a hard spot, and you stopped it. You might have still been able to throw the guy out. And even if you didn't, you would have stopped any other runners from scoring. It was a good play."

Noah smiled. "Okay."

He tossed the ball back. I slipped my glove off, put the ball in its pocket, and stuck it under my arm.

"Hey, want an ice cream?"

"Sure!"

"Grab a seat on the bench over there. I'll be right back." I pointed to the wrought iron bench that Susan and I had placed just off the sidewalk so that we could sit and look at the garden in the evening. Noah walked over and sat down. I went into the house through the back door and returned with two ice cream bars. I handed one to Noah as I sat down.

"Summer League is coming up in a few weeks. That'll be fun. You'll get to play real games."

"Yeah, I guess so." He shrugged and squinted at the same time.

"For a guy who likes baseball, you don't seem very excited about it."

"Yeah, I dunno."

I could see the look behind the eyes again, like there was something profound that he wasn't sure he wanted to let out. I decided to wait it out. We both continued eating our ice cream. A piece of chocolate fell off the side of mine onto the ground.

"Well, now I guess the ants will get some too," I said.

Noah smiled. I looked at him and my eyes caught his for a moment.

"I guess I'm not sure I want to play this year," Noah said.

"That's okay. Why not?"

"I dunno. I didn't play much last year. I wasn't very good. But it was still fun cuz my dad came to watch. But this year—"

"Yeah, I get it. You miss your dad. I'd love to come watch you play. But I know that's not the same. But there is something I've been wanting to tell you."

"What?"

"Well, you really like baseball, right?"

"Yup."

"A lot, right?"

"Yeah."

"Well, not everyone who plays baseball is a real baseball player. Some people just play at baseball, like it's any other game. But real baseball players—the ones who love the game— they play by a code. I call it the Baseball Code. My dad taught it to me, and if you want, I'll teach it to you."

"Will it help me play better?"

"Yes. It will. But it will help you with other things too."

"What kind of code is it? Is it like signals, like when to steal and stuff?"

"No. It's a way of playing the game. But it's more than that. It's a way of doing lots of things."

"Okay. Can you teach me?"

"Yeah, but not all at once. I'll tell you the first part, and we'll work on that. Okay?"

"Okay."

"The first part of the Baseball Code is 'Always work hard. Always do your best.'"

"But don't we do that now when we play catch and practice grounders?"

"Yeah. We do. But can you repeat what I just told you, the first part of the Baseball Code?"

"Always work hard. Do your best."

"Almost. It's *Always* work hard. *Always* do your best. Now try it again."

"*Always* work hard. *Always* do your best."

"Now, it doesn't say just when you're practicing baseball, does it?"

"Nope."

"So where else might you need to always work hard and always do your best?"

Noah shrugged and squinted at the same time again.

"I dunno."

I was feeling pretty comfortable with Noah now, so I gave him a look that matched my tone of disbelief.

"Really?"

"Well, school, I guess."

"That makes sense. And is there a particular class you could work harder in?"

"Math. But I don't like math. I like baseball. Isn't the Baseball Code about baseball. I can work hard at that. It's fun. But I hate doing math."

"That's not how it works. The code is 'Always work hard; always do your best.' You don't get to pick and choose. Doing your best is like a muscle you strengthen or a habit you develop. If you get lazy in one area, you start to get lazy in other areas too. So here's the deal. Tomorrow, when you come to play catch, bring your math homework with you. I'll help you with both—math and baseball. Okay?"

"Okay, Mr. Richards."

"And, enough with the 'Mr. Richards' stuff. It's too formal. Since I'm helping you with baseball, how about you just call me 'Coach.'"

I gave his shoulder a slight shake with my hand as I stood up.

"See you tomorrow," I said, "Don't forget your math book."

Noah said "Okay" and took off across the lawn toward the gate. Then he stopped and turned around.

"Coach?"

"Yeah."

"Do you think I'm a real baseball player?"

I smiled at him.

"I do."

9

Susan and I were married in the spring. It was a simple wedding. There was no sit-down meal or elaborate decoration. The women from our church baked zucchini and pumpkin bread to go along with the wedding cake at the reception. We didn't need fanfare to make the day special. It was special because it was what we wanted in the most sincere and truest sense of the word. It was special because it was a bright sunny day, and all our friends were there.

I was nervous—not because I was worried about taking such a big step. I wasn't worried about whether I was making the right choice. I wasn't worried about what would be next, about what life would be like, or about how things would turn out in the end. None of that bothered me in the slightest. I knew Susan was the one. I knew I was committed. I loved the idea of being married.

I know that sounds naive. But it wasn't. It wasn't that I didn't know there would be bumps and stumbles along the way. I was certain there would be. But somehow I could just see my way through all that. I knew that together we were going to build something lasting, something good.

And I wasn't nervous because I was running away from anything. I had loved my high school and college years. I went to a small, private high school where I made close, enduring friendships. I played baseball and football, and I sang in the choir. I would have been happy if high school had never ended. It was one of the happiest periods of my life.

College moved in a different direction because I went to a large, state school. But that provided me the opportunity to become more engaged in our church group, which was wonderful in its own way. And that was where I met Susan.

So I wasn't nervous because I was worried about the future or because I was running from the past. I was nervous because I had written a song for Susan, and I was going to sing it at the ceremony accompanied by my guitar. I had played guitar and sung in a kind of folk-rock group in high school, and I accompanied choruses at our church. But I hadn't usually sung solos.

Plus, I hadn't told Susan about it. I managed to hide it in the order of service. At one place, it just said "Special Music—*The Lord's Prayer*." That was going to be sung by a friend of ours. But right after that, one of the groomsmen was going to hand me my guitar, and I was going to put the strap over my shoulders and sing what I had written.

As the last notes of *The Lord's Prayer* slowly died out, I stepped over and took the guitar from my friend. My hands were shaking so much that I could barely get the strap over my shoulders without dropping it. I remember thinking that this was going to be a disaster.

Then I turned toward Susan. I saw the look of surprise in her eyes and the slight smile breaking across her face. I played the first chord, and somehow something that I still consider magical or mystical came over me. My nervousness disappeared, and I played and sang like no one else was there. It was perfect.

It was a traditional service for the most part. But it was still the seventies—hence my guitar. And we did write our own vows. We were determined, however, that we weren't going to say things off the cuff like we had heard so often, stuff like, "Oh, I love you so much; I'm so glad I found you. You make me so happy, etc." We wanted our vows to be unique but also poetic and to connect to the meaningful traditions that had come before us and of which we were about to become a part.

So we worked hard at our vows. And we didn't use them in place of, but in addition to the traditional. So when we had each spoken our own, the minister told us to remain facing each other with our hands joined and then asked us,

Do you commit yourself to one another in marriage,
   To have and to hold;
   To love and to cherish;
   For richer or for poorer;
   In sickness and in health;
   From this day forward, as long as you both shall live.

We both smiled and said,
   "I do."

PART IV

THE DIAMOND

10

I was sitting on the bench looking at the rose garden. Students always asked the same questions about math. "When am I ever going to use this?" Or "what is math good for anyway?" I didn't refuse to answer the questions or chide them for asking. After all, education is about asking questions—not just the questions the teacher wants you to ask but the questions *you* want to ask. I'd been at it long enough to have plenty of answers. Math is useful to everyone in one form or another.

But math isn't fundamentally about usefulness, about adding things up or measuring their length. Math is about beauty. It's about the symmetry we see in the world around us every day. Roses are a good example. Each petal is shaped the same and equally spaced around a central point. This is called radial symmetry. Mathematics has developed an entire area of study around the symmetry of roses called "rose curves." But one doesn't have to be an expert in "rose curves" to appreciate the beauty of a rose. We just intuitively appreciate symmetry, whether we're hanging pictures on a wall, admiring the facets of a diamond, or judging which face seems friendlier.

I was waiting for Noah. It was past time for school to be out.

This was going to be our first afternoon working on math together. So I knew I was going to get the question again, and I was prepared. I stood up, walked over to the garden, and picked up the bag of rose food that I had been working into the soil around the roses. As I started back to the garage, I heard feet coming through the side yard, followed closely by what was becoming a familiar voice.

"Hi Coach."

"Hi Noah."

"Ya wanna play some catch?"

"Sure. But we've got something else to do first. Did you bring your math book with you?"

"Yeah . . . well, it's not really a book. It's just a sheet. It's in my backpack."

"Okay. Let's go in the house and use the table."

Noah followed me into the garage. I stashed the rose food under the workbench. Then I opened the door to the house and held it for Noah.

"We'll use the table over there." I pointed to the dining room table that was off to my right.

"Take your backpack off and get your homework out. I've gotta wash my hands."

I turned on the tap in the kitchen sink, poured out some liquid soap, and began to work the dirt out from under my fingernails. I yelled to Noah,

"Go ahead and grab a seat. How was school today?"

"Okay."

I picked up a couple of pencils and some paper. Noah had sat down with his back to the window, so I sat across from him where I could look out into the backyard.

"So what's your homework?"

"Fractions and decimals."

"That's cool. Can I see it?"

"Yeah, I guess . . ."

I could feel it coming. Not only because I saw the look in his eyes, but because I had been here so many times before. He pulled the homework sheet out of his backpack.

"But . . ."

"But what?"

"But, I mean, I get the Baseball Code and everything— 'always do your best.' But what's the point to fractions. When will I ever use this stuff?"

"Okay. Put your homework sheet down. I've got a question for you."

"What?"

"Who's your favorite ball player?"

"Trea Turner."

I tried to hide my failure to recognize the name. I was woefully out of touch with the contemporary heroes of the game.

"What's his batting average?"

"298."

"That's pretty good. So how did you figure that out?"

"I dunno. They just tell you."

"Yeah, I know. But how do THEY figure it out so they can tell you?"

"I dunno. One of the kids at school said that they give you points for all your hits, like one point for a base hit and two points for a double and four points for a home run. Then you just add them up."

"Nope. That's not how they do it. But I can show you how. You want me to?"

"Sure."

"Okay."

I picked up my pencil and slid a piece of paper in front of me.

"Let's say that you were up to bat eight times and you got two hits. Okay?"

"Okay."

"So you write a fraction like this:"

"The '2' on the top stands for the number of hits and the '8' on the bottom stands for the number of times you were up to bat. Got it?"

"Yeah."

"Okay. Now, you change it to a decimal. Do you know how to do that?"

"Not really."

"Well, you divide the number on the bottom into the number on the top, like this:"

I slowly worked the long division problem, asking Noah about each step.

$$\begin{array}{r} .250 \\ 8\overline{\smash{)}2.0} \\ \underline{16} \\ 40 \\ \underline{40} \end{array}$$

"And there's your batting average—250."

"Really?"

"Yup. That's how all the batting averages are figured out for all the players, including Trea Turner. It's all fractions and decimals."

"Wow. That's pretty cool."

"Yeah. It is. So grab your homework, and let's get working on those fractions and decimals. Then you can show the kids at school how batting averages work."

"Okay."

We finished up the homework sheet in about half an hour, and then went out into the backyard to play some catch. After we warmed up, I started throwing Noah some grounders.

"What position does Trea Turner play?"

I was hoping he wouldn't notice that I should already have known this.

"He played shortstop this year. But last year he played second for a while."

I threw a grounder pretty hard, dead center at his feet. At the last second, he stuck out his glove and looked away. The ball bounced over his glove and hit him the stomach.

"Ow!"

I took a step toward Noah to see if he was hurt; he wasn't. He stepped forward, picked up the ball, and threw it back.

"Ya gotta keep your eyes on the ball," I said, holding on to the ball for the moment.

"I know, but it was coming fast. I didn't wanna get hit in the face."

"I get that. But you don't avoid getting hit by not looking. If you keep your eyes on the ball, you can protect yourself. If you're looking, when it bounces toward your face, your hands will automatically move up to protect you." I motioned with my hands to make my point.

"And you'll turn your head at the last second if you need to. But if you turn away before it comes, like you did, then you're more likely to get hit. *Always* keep your eyes on the ball."

"Is that part of the Baseball Code?"

I laughed.

"No. But it's sure part of playin' good baseball. Okay, here it comes. Eyes on the ball."

I tossed one high up into the air so that he had to back up a few steps and wait for it to come down. We played for a while longer. Then I caught the ball, held it, and said,

"C'mere. Let's sit down for a bit."

I walked over to the bench by the rose garden and pushed myself into one corner. Noah sat down on the other end, swung his feet around up on the bench, and pulled his knees up.

"I've got a question for you," I said. "What do you think is beautiful?"

I was looking directly at him. He had his head tilted down toward his knees, so all I could see was his dark brown hair. He didn't respond right way, so I repeated the question.

"What do you think is—"

Noah's head popped up, and he looked right at me.

"Cindy Conner."

"WHAT?" I leaned forward with a quizzical stare. Then I burst into laughter. It got Noah laughing too. After a few seconds, I said,

"I'm not talking about girls, you crazy boy!"

I couldn't help myself. I started laughing again. We both did. I got control and asked,

"Is Cindy Conner a girl in your class?"

"Yeah."

"Okay. I'm not talking about people. I mean, what *things* do you think are beautiful, you know, like roses." I pointed to the rose garden.

"Oh, yeah. I guess roses are beautiful."

"No. You don't get to use my example. You have to . . . Oh, forget it. I'm just fishing."

"Fishing? What d'ya mean?"

"It's just something that teachers sometimes say. It means I was trying to get you to say something that I should have just told you myself. In other words, I was fishing for an answer that I already knew. Here, I've got something for you."

I reached under the bench and pulled out a book that I had bought and put there earlier. It was a large, picture book of famous baseball stadiums around the country. On the front cover was a picture of Fenway Park in Boston, one of the most iconic ballparks of all time. I handed it to Noah.

"Wow. That's cool. Thanks!"

"It's something that I think is beautiful. It has pictures of all the ball fields where the major teams play. When I was your age, there was nothing as beautiful to me as a baseball field— the perfect diamond made by the smooth, brown dirt of the base paths with the square white bases at the corners; the green grass of the infield, and the huge, green expanse of the outfield flowing in all directions."

Noah was already flipping through the pictures in the book.

"I think they're beautiful too," he said.

"When my parents took me somewhere in the car, I looked out the window at the scenery, and whenever I saw an open field, I tried to imagine if it was big enough for a baseball field. Hand me the book for a second. I wanna tell you something else about math."

Noah handed the book back to me. I closed it and pointed to the baseball diamond in Fenway Park on the cover.

"See this ball diamond?"

"Yup."

"It's really just a square that's been turned up on one point, right?"

As I asked, I turned the cover so that I was holding the first base line flat along the edge of the bench.

"Oh, yeah, I see."

"So one side of the square is from home to first, the next side is from first to second," I traced the base paths with my finger as I talked, "the next from second to third, and the last from third to home. And each side is the same length—90 feet —a perfect square."

"Yeah."

"And that's part of what makes it beautiful. When you stand at home plate in the batter's box, and you look at the pitcher, you see second base straight behind him. Then when you look to your right, you see first base 90 feet away. But if you look to your left, you see third base exactly the same way. Everything's even. One side reflects the other. The same with left field and right field. And here's the thing. You've talked about squares in math class, right?"

"Sure."

"That's because math is the language we use to describe things that are beautiful. Of course, we also use math to do practical things like figure out batting averages. But the more important thing that math does is describe those things that we think are beautiful, like squares and diamonds and circles and baseballs and roses."

"It doesn't seem like that in math class."

"I know. But that's just because you haven't gotten to the best part yet. You have to trust me on this one. So remember when you're doing your math homework that math helps us to describe what's beautiful, like roses and baseball."

Noah smiled, "And Cindy Conner."

"Okay." I laughed, "if you say so. Let's play some more catch."

11

My dad and I climbed into our light green '61 VW Bug and headed toward the Ventura Freeway. I was so excited I could hardly contain myself. We were going to a Dodger game. When we lived in New York, we were upstate in a small town. So we never ventured into the city to go to a major-league ball game. This was my first.

"Hey, Dad."

"Yup."

"Koufax is pitching tonight!"

"I know. That's why I chose tonight for your first game."

"I'll bet he's gonna strike out a bunch—maybe more than ten. He throws really fast."

"That's true. But he's also got a great curve. That's what keeps 'em guessing."

I loved talking baseball with my dad. It felt like we were pals. He followed the Dodgers almost as closely as I did. The difference was that he'd read about the games the next day in the newspaper. I listened to them live on the radio as I was falling to sleep at night. I had a white, plastic-faced radio that set in the headboard of my bed. I'd tune it to KFI and listen as

Vin Scully announced the games. Scully was great. I loved how when someone hit a home run, he'd say, "She's back, she's a way back, she's gone!"

"What's it like to be in a big league stadium?" I asked.

"There's a lot of noise from the crowd. Lots of cheering. You'll find out pretty soon. We're getting there early so we can watch some batting practice."

"That's so cool. I wanna see Frank Howard or Tommy Davis hit a home run. Where are we sitting?"

"Our seats are on the second tier along the third base side."

"I brought my mitt. Do you think I could catch a foul ball?"

"It's possible. But don't set your heart on it. It would have to be hit right at you, and there'll be a lot of other folks trying to catch it."

"I know. But I'm gonna try. I can't wait. This is so great."

We whizzed down the Ventura Freeway to the Hollywood Freeway and then to the Pasadena Freeway. But I wasn't really paying attention to how we got there. I just wanted to be there already, watching my favorite players in person for the first time.

"I'll bet Wills steals a couple of bases."

"That wouldn't surprise me."

"He's so fast. I love the way he slides. Go Maury! Go! Go! Go!" I chanted the words that the crowd at the stadium would scream every time Maury Wills got on base.

My dad smiled.

"Hey, can we get a hotdog at the ballpark?"

"I doubt it. Food is overpriced at games. Maybe some peanuts."

"How about a hamburger on the way home?"

"We'll see."

We pulled into the parking area and followed the waving arms of the parking attendants to our parking slot. There were special lots for season ticket holders, but for the rest of us, it was park and hike.

We walked a long way to the stadium. Then we walked more, up flights of stairs, following the signs to our section. Like my dad said, we had gotten there early to watch batting practice, but crowds of fans were already pouring in. My excitement was growing by the minute.

Then it happened.

I had just turned from the wide entry aisle to start walking down toward our seats when I caught my first glimpse. There was the baseball diamond, surrounded by gray steel and cement, like a brilliant green flower bursting through a hole in the sidewalk. I hadn't imagined how big or bright it would be.

It was overwhelming—the rich, perfectly trimmed grass of the infield, bounded by the dark brown base paths running at right angles from home plate. And the outfield just went on forever, a never-ending sea of green. You could have put three little league fields in it. Ball players with clean, white uniforms were everywhere, all over the field. I could see myself down there—running, throwing, catching. You could hear the crack of the bat from the guys taking batting practice.

"Hey," Dad said, "Are ya gonna keep moving so we can get to our seats?"

I hadn't even noticed that I had stopped walking and was standing still, gazing out at the field.

"Oh, yeah, sure," I said.

We got to our row and scooted into our seats.

"Hey, Dad, look there's Frank Howard right there! He's gonna take batting practice. This is so cool."

We watched batting practice. I got to see Frank Howard and Tommy Davis hit some into the bleachers. I saw Maury Wills warming up along the sidelines. I even caught a glimpse of Don Drysdale. Just before the game was going to start, my dad bought us each a bag of peanuts. They were the kind in the shells that you had to crack open. This was the best night ever.

Then Koufax took the mound. I loved to watch Koufax pitch. When he wound up, his left hand with the ball went so far back it almost touched the ground. Then he stretched his right leg forward, pushed off the rubber with his left, and flung the ball right up over the top. It was like watching a human catapult.

In the first inning, he threw just nine pitches. That was it! Nine straight strikes. Then he turned around and walked back to the dugout. I had never even heard of anything like that. We all knew that something amazing was going to happen. Inning after inning went by with the Mets not getting a hit. I was on the edge of my seat.

In the seventh, after we had all sung "Take Me Out to the Ball Game," Frank Howard even hit a home run. I couldn't believe it. It was just what I'd been hoping for. But in the bottom of the eighth, Koufax was set to be the leadoff hitter. I turned to my dad,

"Koufax isn't a very good hitter. You don't think the coach will pull him out of the game, do ya, even though he's got a no-hitter goin', like that other guy you told me about?"

My dad smiled, "Nope. He won't because they're ahead five to nothing. So the coach isn't worried about getting any extra runs."

"Phew, I'm glad," I said, "that would be terrible."

"It sure would."

Koufax came up and struck out looking.

In the top of the ninth, Koufax walked the first batter. The next two grounded out, and there we were—the whole stadium holding its breath, waiting for the last out. It took four pitches, but finally, the batter hit a ground ball to Wills at short. He fielded it, tossed it to second, and it was over.

The place erupted. All the players mobbed Koufax.

Everyone in the stadium was yelling and cheering and waving hats and gloves and programs and anything else they could get their hands on. And the cushions started flying. People rented blue cushions to put on the hard seats. My dad and I didn't rent any. But those who did sailed them from the stands onto the field like frisbees. The field was littered with them.

It was beautiful.

It was a long walk back to the car, a long line to get out of the parking lot, and a long ride home. But I chattered at my dad most of the way. Finally, however, I couldn't hold out any longer, and I fell to sleep.

"Hey," my dad was shaking my shoulder, "you still want that hamburger?"

I pulled my head up, blinked a couple of times, and looked around. We were sitting in front of a Bob's Big Boy.

"Sure," I said.

We went in and sat down at the counter and ordered burgers and fries. I could barely keep my eyes open long enough to eat. But there was no way I was going to miss this. It was the perfect ending to a perfect day.

I turned to my dad and said,

"Can you believe it, Dad? Koufax threw a no-hitter!"

"He sure did."

12

I hadn't seen Noah for a while. We'd been working on math and playing catch almost every afternoon. He caught on to math quickly. In fact, he picked up math more quickly than baseball, although I'd never tell him that. He was doing well at both. But then he just stopped coming by. I hadn't seen him since last Tuesday.

The Presbyterian Church was only a few blocks away. Most Sundays I walked. Sometimes I sat after the service and listened to the organ. Some people don't like organ music, but I do. So did Susan. The church had a great old pipe organ. I was amazed at the coordination it took to play several different keyboards as well as a pedalboard with one's feet. Even the loud pieces with all the stops out were somehow soothing. The music transported me to a different time and place.

I had just gotten up, shaken Pastor Thompson's hand, and was walking down the front steps when I saw Ashley turn down the sidewalk ahead of me. I hurried to catch up with her, stumbling off the last step and just catching myself before I fell. I called out,

"Hey Ashley, mind if I walk along?"

She stopped and turned around.

"Oh, hi Terry. Sure. How are you doing?"

I caught up alongside, and we continued walking.

"That was a nice service today," I said, "I like to sit and listen to the organ afterwards."

"Really? It's so loud. I kinda wish they'd just use the piano. I've got this friend who goes to a church where they have a band with guitars and stuff. I went with her once. That was really fun. But this is so convenient, you know, I can walk and everything."

"Yeah. Right. Hey, I was wondering how Noah was doing. He'd been coming by after school to get help with math and to play catch. But the last few days he just stopped coming. I wondered if he was sick or something."

"Oh, yeah, I've been meaning to call you and say thanks for helping him, really. He started doing so much better in school, especially math. He seemed to take a special interest in that. I really appreciate it."

"No need to thank me. I enjoy helping him. It makes me feel like a teacher again."

We stepped off the curb and walked across the street.

"And like I told you before, it gives me a chance to throw the ball around. It's good for me. I was just worried when he stopped coming by that something might be wrong."

"Well, to be really honest, there is. I mean, he's not sick or anything. It's his father. You know we're divorced, right?"

"Yeah."

"Well, when Frank—that's his father—used to live close, Noah saw him on weekends."

"Yeah, I remember seeing him around from time to time."

"Right. But then last winter, he took a new job in New York. He's an attorney, and he took a job with some large firm there. I tried to persuade him not to go, you know, because of Noah.

But he said it was a really good opportunity that he couldn't pass up.

"So Noah was supposed to fly out there to see him over spring break. But at the last minute, Frank said that he had a case in court and Noah couldn't come. So he made plans to come out here next week. He was going to take Noah to the beach and to Disneyland. Then he called last Tuesday evening and said that he'd been assigned a new case and that he didn't have time to come.

"I really don't know what to do. Noah is so disappointed. He's been looking forward to this for so long. Like I said, he was doing so well, but now I can barely get him to go to school, let alone do anything else. That's why I left him home this morning. It's so close and only for an hour, so I thought he'd be okay. I just needed to come."

Ashley had stopped walking and turned toward me as she explained the situation. There was obvious emotion in her voice and face. When she finished, she turned back and started walking again.

"I'm so sorry," I said, "I had no idea. If there's anything I can do, please let me know."

"I don't know. I mean, he really loved playing catch with you. He talked about the baseball thing all the time and looked at that book you gave him. He probably just needs some time."

"He did tell me once that he missed his dad. But I didn't ask him anything more about it. I didn't want to pry."

"No. It's not your problem, really. I just wanted you to know that he's not sick or anything. He's just having a hard time."

"Right, of course."

We walked along in silence for a couple of blocks. When we got to her house, we stopped. I turned and said,

"Well, have a good week. Thanks for letting me know about Noah. Say 'hi' to him for me."

"I will. You have a good week too."

I turned to continue on, but then turned back.

"Hey," I added, "I'm planting a couple of new roses tomorrow afternoon. Would you mind telling Noah that I could use some help?"

"Sure. I'll let him know."

"Okay. Thanks."

I headed for home. I could turn the baseball game on. Or maybe I'd get in the car and go get a cup of coffee.

I was sitting in my chair reading and listening to Yo-Yo Ma play Bach's Unaccompanied Cello Suites. I wasn't highbrow. Neither was Susan. But Susan played the piano, and so she knew something about classical music. So she had introduced me to some of the familiar, well-loved pieces. Of course, we also listened to the Beatles, Simon and Garfunkel, and the Eagles. But Yo-Yo Ma playing Bach, I had to admit. There was something magical about it.

It was just about time. I set my book down, picked up my phone, and hit the stop button on the music. I had all day, of course. But I'd been waiting till now to take the roses, shovel, and potting soil out into the backyard with the hope that Noah might drop by to help.

I went out into the garage, threw everything into the wheelbarrow, and pushed it to the side of the rose garden. I took the shovel and dug out the old rose bushes so I'd be ready to put the new ones in. Then I sat down on the bench to wait.

The roses I was replacing hadn't been doing well for the last six months or so. I didn't know why. The truth is that I wasn't a great gardener. I didn't mind working in the rose garden, but I didn't know a lot about it. I had done some reading. But nothing I did seemed to help.

I looked across at the rose in the center. It had a couple of small red blooms that were starting to wilt and a bud or two. It wasn't flourishing either. But that one was staying put. That's all there was to it. Maybe a little more rose food around the base.

"Hey Mr. Richards, I mean, Coach."

I startled a little and turned to my left.

"Hi Noah. It's good to see you."

Noah had on blue jeans and his Jurassic Park T-shirt.

"Yeah. My mom told me you needed some help."

"That's right. I'm replacing a couple of roses. It's always easier with two people. Grab one of the rose bushes from the wheelbarrow over there and set it by the garden here. Hold the plastic can around the bottom, and watch out for the thorns."

While Noah was carrying the rose over, I grabbed some pruning shears. Then I started cutting the plastic can away from the roots.

"So what have you been up to?"

"Nothin'"

"How's the math goin'?"

"Okay."

I threw the plastic can onto the ground. Then I stepped over into the garden and set the rose into one of the holes left from the bushes I had taken out.

"Okay, Noah. Now go get that bag of potting soil from the wheelbarrow."

Noah brought the bag over.

"Now, pour some of the soil into the hole all around the rose. Fill it up about half-way."

Noah lifted up the bag. He turned it quickly almost upside down, and a large amount of soil spilled out into one side of the hole.

"Whoa!" I said. "Slow it down there."

He tipped the bag back up.

"Sorry."

"That's okay. Just push the dirt all around until it's even. . . .

Yeah. That's right. Okay, now gently push in the dirt that's mounded up all around the hole."

"Like that?" Noah pushed the remaining dirt in until it was smooth with the surface of the garden.

"Perfect," I said. "All right, one down, one to go."

We planted the second rose. This time, Noah didn't need me to tell him what to do. He had it down. When we were finished, I stood up and said,

"Look at that! We planted two roses. Not a bad afternoon's work. Thanks for the help."

"Sure."

"Hey, ya wanna play some catch?"

"I didn't bring my mitt."

"I've got an extra in the garage, or you could run home and get yours."

"Yeah, maybe."

"Let me put this stuff away."

I loaded the potting soil, the cut up plastic cans, the shovel, and my pruning shears into the wheelbarrow and headed toward the garage. I pushed the wheelbarrow through the door and left it setting by the workbench. Then I grabbed my glove and ball and the extra glove and went back out.

I thought maybe Noah would already have taken off home to get his mitt. But he was still sitting on the bench like he had the other day with his knees pulled up against his chest and his head down.

"Hey, are ya ready to play?"

"I dunno."

"I've got an extra—"

"He's not coming."

"What?"

I walked over and sat down on the other side of the bench, pushing myself into the corner so I was facing Noah.

"He's not coming."

"Who's not coming?"

Noah still had his head down on top of his knees.

"My dad. He said he was going to come see me. But he's not. I don't think he wants to."

"Hey, buddy, look. Look up here for a second."

Noah looked up. He was sniffling, and under the brown hair falling across his forehead, a tear was running down his cheek.

"Listen, man, I don't think that's true. I'm sure he wants to. What did he say?"

"He said his boss gave him a new case, and he didn't have time."

"Okay."

"Yeah, but he was s'posed to come before, and he didn't. Now he's not again. I don't think he wants to."

"Listen, buddy, he's a lawyer, right?"

"Yup."

"And you said his boss gave him a new case?"

"Yeah."

"Okay. Here's the thing. I'm going to tell you something else about the Baseball Code."

"The Baseball Code? We're not playin' baseball."

"True. But the Baseball Code isn't just about baseball, right? Remember, it was also about math, about always doing your best."

"But I did my best, and my dad still isn't coming."

"Okay. But there's more to the Baseball Code than just doing your best. So what's the Baseball Code so far, the part that I told you?"

"Always work hard. Always do your best."

"Right. So here's the next part. 'Always play fair. Always put the team first.'"

Noah just looked at me.

"So you know what it means to play fair, right?"

"Yeah."

"Well, I'm gonna tell you about what it means to 'always put the team first.' When I was your age, I played baseball in Little League. It was like your Summer League. I wanted to play second base, but my coach put me in center field. I told my dad that it wasn't fair because I was as good at second base as anyone else on the team."

"Were you as good?"

"I was, maybe better."

"Then it wasn't fair."

"Well, you have to listen to the rest of the story. My dad said that maybe my coach needed me in center field because I was really fast and no one on the team could run down fly balls like I could. He had other kids who could play second base okay, but he didn't have anyone who could play center field good enough except for me.

"So my dad told me that even though I wanted to play second base, maybe I should be happy playing center field for the good of the team. Baseball isn't about what one player wants to do. It's about the whole team. That's why the Baseball Code says 'always put the team first.'"

"Okay, so?"

"Well, your dad works for a law firm, a company, right?"

"Yeah."

"That's his team. His boss is like the coach. Maybe the boss knows that he needs your dad to work on this case right now because there's no one else who can do it as good as he can. Your dad would like to come out here and see you. That's what he'd rather do, just like I wanted to play second base. But he has to do what's best for his team."

"Do you really think so?"

"Of course I do. Before your dad moved, didn't he come and see you on the weekends?"

"Yup."

"So there's no reason to think that has changed. He probably feels as bad as you do that he can't come. He just has to do what's best for his team right now. I'm sure he'll come later."

"Yeah, probably."

"So what's the Baseball Code? Always work hard ... "

"Always do your best."

"And ... "

"Always play fair. Always put the team first."

"You got it!"

Noah wiped his eyes with the insides of his fists.

"Hey," I said, "Have you ever been to a Dodger game?"

"No."

"Would you like to go?"

"Really?"

A smile started to break out across his face.

"Really. There's nothing like seeing one of those baseball diamonds in the book I gave you in real life. The first time I walked into Dodger Stadium, I couldn't believe my eyes."

"Is it beautiful?"

"It sure is."

PART V

SWING AND A MISS

13

When I left the post office, I was annoyed. It wasn't that it mattered exactly when the package I was sending would get there. It didn't. It was that I'd handed the window clerk a prepaid priority mail envelope. After I swiped my card, I asked him when he thought the package might arrive. "Oh, I'd give it four or five days," he said. He was standing right in front of a poster that read, "Priority Mail—Delivery in 1 to 3 business days." It was Monday.

I didn't argue. Instead, as I walked out the door, I was inventing new slogans, like "The U. S. Post Office—Sooner or later, we'll get it there!" I taught math. It seemed to me that a little precision in communication couldn't hurt. I mean, I couldn't get away with telling students that four divided by two was somewhere between one and three or with handing out a study sheet that said Pi = 3.14, and then when a student asked me its value responding, "Oh, I'd say somewhere around 4 or 5."

Susan would have told me that I was becoming a curmudgeon, that I should let it go, that "it is what it is." I couldn't argue with that either. I climbed behind the wheel, backed up the car, and pulled out onto the street.

I was late for my appointment with Pastor Thompson. When I got to the church, he saw me through his window as I was walking in and waved me on into his office.

"Hello John," I said.

"Hi TR. Have a seat. We haven't chatted in a while. How have you been?"

John Thompson was much younger than me, somewhere in his forties. He was easy-going, almost flippant at times. But he was genuine. I trusted him despite his youthfulness. He was someone I could talk to.

"I'm doing all right," I said, "keeping busy. How's the family?"

"They're all fine. You know, I see you sometimes on Sundays, but that's about it. George told me you haven't been coming to small group meetings. I called you a few times. But I didn't hear back. Is something going on?"

If it had been anyone but John, I'd have already been out the door. I hated prying questions.

"Yeah. Sorry about that. I actually meant to call you back. But look, John, I didn't really come here to talk about me. I have a practical reason. I — "

John cut me off.

"Sure, Terry, we'll have time to talk about whatever that is. But I am a little worried about you. You know, you can't just bottle everything up inside. It's not helpful. The last time I talked with you, you were still pretty angry."

"Well, yeah, of course. But that's getting better. I mean, I still am at times, but I think I'm feeling my way."

John smiled and rocked back in his chair.

"What does that mean?"

I smiled too, and said,

"I don't know, John, I'm not a theologian. I'm a mathematician."

"That didn't clarify things for me."

I had to laugh out loud.

"Okay. Well, you know that Susan and I met at church, right?"

"Yeah."

"So, church, God, faith—they were always part of our lives, like the air we breathed. I never really thought much about it. Then it happened. Something as random as a blood clot. I was angry. It didn't make sense to me. I couldn't explain it.

"My whole life as a math teacher was about figuring things out, about proofs and explanations. I had a colleague who used to say that theologians were just sloppy mathematicians. That resonated with me. It seemed like people who accepted things without a reason were just sloppy or lazy. There had to be an explanation. But the more I looked for one, the more angry I got. I just couldn't figure things out."

John rocked forward, placed his elbows on the desk and looked straight at me.

"So did you figure something out? Is that why I haven't heard from you?"

"Mmm, no, actually something you said in a sermon pushed me in a different direction."

"Really."

"You were talking about Job, how all these terrible things happened to him, and how he knows he's innocent. So he begs for an audience with God, to present his case, and God grants it to him. But then God doesn't answer his questions. He doesn't even really listen to him. God just asks him a bunch of questions he can't answer."

"I don't recall that being one of my best sermons. How did it help?"

"It was the first question God asked Job, in chapter 38. I don't have it memorized. Do you have a bible?"

John smiled. "I think I could scare one up."

He reached over his desk, picked up his bible and handed to to me.

I turned to the chapter and looked for the verse.

"Okay, here it is. 'Where were you when I laid the foundation of the earth? Tell me, if you have understanding. . . . when the morning stars sang together, and all the heavenly beings shouted for joy?'

"It reminded me of something that happened at work. One day when I was still teaching, in the lunchroom, someone from the physics department was talking about the Theory of Everything. Then this woman from philosophy asked, 'If someone were to discover this Theory of Everything, would it resolve the Israeli/Palestinian problem in the Middle East?' Of course, the physicist said 'No.' She replied, 'Then why do you call it the Theory of Everything?' I guess it reminded me of how much we don't and can't know."

John leaned back in his chair again and laughed.

"But there was something about the end of the verse too," I said, "how 'the morning stars sang together, and all the heavenly beings shouted for joy.' It made me think that there's a deep joy woven into the fabric of the universe that can't be reached by our understanding, something more mystical.

"Anyway, the more I thought about it, the more I realized I needed to quit looking for an explanation—that it was beyond my understanding. So I did, and I felt better. I'm still angry at times, and sad. But I think I'm moving in the right direction."

John nodded like he was thinking about what I'd said. Then he just sat and looked at me until it got a little uncomfortable. Finally, he said,

"You do know you can call me any time, right?"

"Of course."

"Okay, TR, what is it you came to talk about?"

"Right. You know that field behind the church with the old broken-down backstop?"

"Yeah."

"Well, it doesn't seem like anyone uses it. I've been helping Ashley's son, Noah, with baseball. So I was wondering if we could use that to practice hitting and fielding. I think if I mowed the grass and weeds, it'd be fine, and the backstop would be helpful for batting practice."

"Sure. I don't know why not. I think back when the church had a younger congregation, they used it for softball games. But I haven't seen anyone out there for years. The weeds are pretty high, though. Do you need some help?"

"I don't need any help mowing. The one thing I've got a lot of is time. But I'd be grateful if I could use the church's mower. That way I wouldn't have to lug mine back and forth."

"No problem. I can't vouch for how great a condition it's in. But it's in the shed behind the church. I've got an extra key right here."

He opened a desk drawer, pulled out a key, and handed it to me.

"And don't be a stranger, TR."

"Thanks, John. I won't."

I didn't want to let go of the safety bar because I knew it would mean restarting the mower. But I had to. My back was killing me. So I dropped it, leaned back, and stretched my back out as far as I could. I'd been mowing for a little more than an hour. This was the third day, and I was almost finished.

It was a lot of grass and weeds, and some of it was pretty

tall. So I had to go slowly and then go back over it a couple of times. I wanted to mow what would be the entire outfield so that we wouldn't lose any balls that happened to roll out there from batting and fielding practice. Weeding the base paths so they would be all dirt would have looked better, but I wasn't up to it.

I only worked a couple hours a day. I mowed in the morning because it was cooler. I also wanted to be free in the afternoons to play catch with Noah and help him with his math. He didn't know anything about the field yet. I wanted it to be a surprise, and today was the day.

I had bought brand new bases, a home plate, and a pitching rubber online. The bases were still in the garage, but I had home plate and a small spade with me. The outline where home plate used to be in front of the backstop was still visible. So I dug a shallow hole and set the new plate in place. I stomped on it a few times to make sure it was secure.

Then I pushed the mower back, locked it in the shed behind the church, threw the spade in the trunk, and drove home. When I got there, I loaded up the trunk with the other stuff Noah and I would need to finish the field—the new bases and pitching rubber; a canvas bag with a sports tape measure, a few stakes, a small sledge hammer, and some twine; and a shovel. Then I went in and fixed myself some lunch.

That afternoon, I was sitting on the bench by the rose garden when Noah came around the garage.

"Hi Coach! Math or catch first?"

I stood up and walked toward him.

"Well, neither, exactly. I've got something else in mind."

"What?"

Noah had a look of skeptical surprise on his face, like I was going to ask him to paint the garage.

"You'll see. Mind if we take a short ride?"

"Nope."

Noah turned, and we walked toward the garage. The church wasn't that far away. We could have walked there. But though I was trying to hide it, I was pretty excited, and I didn't want to take the time. We hopped into the car.

"Seatbelt on?" I asked.

"Yup," Noah said as he pulled the belt across his lap and clicked it in place. "Where are we goin'?"

"You'll see."

I backed the car out onto the street. We rode in silence the few blocks to the church where I pulled into the parking lot.

"We're goin' to church?" There was the same squint-eyed, skeptical look I'd just seen earlier.

I laughed. "Nope."

I got out of the car and walked back to the trunk. Noah followed along.

"Then what are we doing here?"

"We're gonna build a baseball field."

"REALLY?" Noah's eyes opened wide.

"Really."

"How do we do that?"

"You'll have to wait and see."

I opened the trunk. We took all the stuff out and started toting it over to the field. It was a lot to carry, so we dropped some things here and there along the way and had to stop to pick them up.

When we got there, we set everything down in front of the backstop.

"Look at that," I said.

"I've seen that old backstop before."

"I'm not talking about the backstop. I'm talking about that."

I pointed in the other direction. Noah turned and noticed home plate for the first time.

"There's a real home plate! And all the grass and weeds are mowed down close. Who did that?"

"I did. And you and I are going to finish it. We're going to put the other bases in. Then we can do more than play catch. We can practice batting, and fielding, and running the bases —everything."

"This is so cool. How do we do it?"

"Well, the first thing we need is one of the stakes out of the bag and the sledge hammer. Can you go get those and bring them to home plate? Just dump the bag out on the ground."

Noah ran over and dumped the bag. Then he grabbed a stake and the sledge hammer. The sledge was heavy, so he struggled a little to get it over to home plate.

"Okay," I said, "We're going to set a stake at the back of the plate. So you hold the stake right at the pointed back end of the plate, and I'll pound it in with the hammer."

Noah held the stake in place, and I swung the hammer. But just before it was going to hit the top of the stake, Noah pulled his hands away. The stake fell over and the hammer swung free in the air.

I laughed.

"Hey, what was that about?"

"I didn't want you to hit me with the hammer."

I laughed again, and it got Noah laughing, too.

"Okay. Look, I'm going to be careful. I've had a lot of practice using a hammer."

I couldn't help but laugh a little again.

"I won't hit your hands. But you've got to hold the stake steady, or it won't work. Okay?"

"Okay, Coach."

Noah picked up the stake and held it back in place.

"Ready?"

"Yup."

He said "Yup," but his face didn't look like he was so sure. I swung the hammer. Noah held on, and the stake bit into the ground. I took a few more swings, and it was fixed.

"Perfect. Okay, Noah, now come get behind the plate. Do you see that the back of the plate is shaped like one corner of a square?"

"Yeah."

"Well. That's one corner of our baseball diamond. So if we start here, and go this way, we have the first base line. Right?"

I took my finger and ran it from the back point of the plate along the right edge and then continued in a straight line for a foot or so, leaving a mark in the dirt.

"Okay," Noah said.

"So we just have to keep that line straight all the way to first base. So grab another stake for us and a roll of twine."

We tied the loose end of the twine around the stake behind home plate. Then we lined the twine up along the angled back edge of the plate and rolled out sixty feet, walking along what would be the first base line. There we pounded another stake into the ground, wrapped the twine twice around the stake, and set the roll down. Then we grabbed another stake and roll of twine and did the same along the third base line.

"Okay," I asked, "Are you ready for a little math?"

"Aren't we going to finish the field first?"

I smiled.

"We are. But we're going to use math to help us figure out where to put second base. I picked up the roll of twine from where we had wrapped it around the stake at third base. I rolled out another sixty feet walking toward first base, cut it, and dropped the end on the ground.

Similarly, I picked up the roll of twine from where we had wrapped it around the stake at first base. I rolled out sixty feet walking toward third base, cut it, and dropped the end on the ground.

Then I had Noah stand about halfway between first and third, and I handed him the ends of both pieces of twine.

"The piece of twine coming from first base is sixty feet long," I said. "That will be the distance between first and second. The piece of twine coming from third base is sixty feet long also. That will be the distance between second and third. Now I want you to hold both ends so they are touching each other and walk toward center field.

"You want to keep walking toward center field until both pieces of twine are tight and the ends are still touching. If one piece of twine starts to get tight before the other, just move away from the one that's looser until it tightens up too. When they're both tight and touching, that's where second base goes."

Noah started walking with me following behind. He followed my instructions well. When both lines were tight with the ends touching, he stopped.

"Are both lines tight?" I asked.

"Yup."

"What would happen if you kept walking?"

"The ends wouldn't touch any more."

"What would have happened if you had stopped before you got where you are?"

"The lines wouldn't be tight."

"That's right. Remember when we talked about how math describes what is beautiful like the baseball diamond or roses?"

"Yeah."

"Well, math does describe what is beautiful. But it also describes what's true. That's how we know where to put second base. Math tells us that if the lines from first and third are both sixty feet long, the distance between the bases, then where the ends are tight and touch has to be the place for second base, the corner of the diamond."

"That's awesome."

"Yeah, it is. Now stay right where you are, and I'll go grab another stake."

We pounded a stake to mark second base. Then we got to digging. We set the anchor plates for the bases and put the bases in place. We set a pitching rubber forty-six feet from home plate. When we were done, we walked to the backstop, leaned back against it, and looked out across the field.

It wasn't Dodger Stadium. It wasn't even the local park. There were no dirt base paths or white painted foul lines down each side. But it was *our* field, and the new, bright home plate was gleaming in the sun.

"Okay, Noah, put the tape measure, stakes, and twine in the bag, and take them back to the car. I'll grab the shovel and the sledge and be right behind you. Third base doesn't look quite right. I'm gonna give it a quick check."

Noah gathered up the stuff and headed to the car. I walked over to third. It looked a little high. I jumped on top of it, and it settled into place. On my way back to get the shovel and sledge, I walked up to the side of the plate and stepped into the imaginary batter's box with my imaginary bat on my shoulder. I gazed out at the fresh white shining bases and across the freshly mowed outfield. I couldn't help myself. I raised my arm, pointed to the fence, and took my swing.

I was hot, tired, and perfectly happy.

14

Our first argument was on our honeymoon. It was my fault. I was a procrastinator. Susan had told me about the place on the coast where she had dreamed about staying since she was a kid. It was beautiful, no doubt about it. Pine covered hills running up from the beach. Rustic rooms with fireplaces, overlooking the ocean. When I called and they told me they were all booked, I didn't know what to do. I made reservations at a place close by with a similar setting. But I knew it wouldn't be the same.

I wasn't so stupid as to let her find out at the last minute. So I told her a couple of weeks before. We were sitting on the couch in her apartment going over plans for the wedding.

"Susan," I said, "I have to tell you something."

"What?"

"I've been planning to go to The Old Camino Lodge for our honeymoon."

Susan smiled and tilted her head back slightly.

"I figured," she said.

"But—" I could barely bring myself to let the next words out of my mouth.

"But I called too late. They were all booked up."

She tried as hard as she could to hide it. But it was impossible. I could see the surge of disappointment.

"That's okay. We'll just pick another place."

"I'm sorry."

I could see she was holding back tears, and that pushed me to the verge as well.

"I'm really sorry. It's all my fault. I—"

My voice broke. I pressed my eyes closed to hold back the emotion. Susan leaned forward and wrapped her arms around me.

"It's okay," she said.

But now she was crying, and so was I.

"I'm so, so sorry."

That, of course, was not the argument. The argument came on the third day of our honeymoon. We were sitting on the deck of the "other place" where I had gotten reservations, watching the breakers roll onto the beach, when Susan said,

"This is probably just as nice as The Old Camino Lodge, don't you think?"

I turned and looked at her.

"Why do you keep doing that?"

"Doing what?"

"You know exactly what I'm talking about."

"No. I don't."

"Yeah, you do. You keep bringing up The Old Camino Lodge. I told you I was sorry about it. What do you want me to do?"

"I'm not asking you to do anything. I like where we are. That's what I said. Are you saying I can't mention The Old Camino Lodge forever just because you made a mistake?"

"I didn't say you couldn't mention it forever. But you keep mentioning it on our honeymoon. That seems like you're throwing it in my face."

"No I'm not. I'm perfectly happy here. You're just being paranoid."

"If you were perfectly happy, you wouldn't keep bringing it up." I could feel my voice getting louder. "I said I was sorry. I wish you would just let it go."

I stood up, opened the sliding glass door that led into our room, and went inside. About fifteen minutes later, Susan came in. I was sitting in an easy chair pouting. She sat down on the side of the bed across from me.

"Look, I said it was okay, and I meant it. I'm not mad about anything. But saying you're sorry doesn't make The Old Camino Lodge disappear or make me forget about it."

"Well, then what's the point of saying you're sorry? If someone forgives you, aren't they supposed to forget about what happened?"

"That's silly. It isn't magic for you to say you're sorry and for me to say it's okay. It doesn't erase my memory. What if I threw a rock at you and put out your eye? I could be truly sorry and tell you so, and you could forgive me. But would that give you your eye back?"

Susan was studying literature. Like our discussion about the nature of love on the beach before we were married, she liked to ponder things philosophically. I had graduated with a math degree and tended to see things more practically—what's the immediate problem to be solved.

"But then why bother to apologize at all?" I asked. "I mean, if it doesn't really change anything."

"I didn't say it didn't change anything," Susan said. "It changes the relationship. When you told me you were sorry about the reservation, and I could see you really meant it, that told me how important I was to you—how much you loved me. Saying you're sorry opens the door to love."

As much as I didn't want to see it, I knew that she had a point. I sat there for a moment. Then I said,

"Okay, I see that."

"And I see what you're saying, too. It's painful to be reminded of something you were sorry about. I won't mention it again while we're on our honeymoon. I'm sorry I upset you."

"Well, I'm sorry about the whole thing."

Susan leaned over and kissed my cheek.

"Let's go for a walk," she said.

15

I knew that Noah would have his mitt in his backpack. So as soon as he showed up after school the next afternoon, I threw mine in the back seat and we took off.

"I can't wait to play on our new field!" Noah said.

"Me, too. It's gonna be a lot of fun. But I've got another surprise for you."

"Really? What is it?"

"You'll see."

"Oh, c'mon. Just tell me."

I pulled the car into the church parking lot and eased it to a stop.

"You'll see in a minute."

We got out of the car, and Noah watched as I opened the trunk.

"Wow! A new bat!" He picked up the bat and swung it through the air.

"And look at all those baseballs!" He turned toward me. "Are those real?"

"They sure are. I'll grab the bucket of balls, you take the bat, and let's go have some batting practice."

We walked over to the field. I carried the bucket of base-balls out to the pitching rubber as Noah took his place at home plate.

"Okay," I said, "get into your stance and get your bat up. Here it comes."

I took a ball out of the bucket, wound up, and threw the first pitch. It bounced a foot in front of the plate and rolled past Noah to the backstop. He instinctively took off after it.

"Noah," I yelled. "don't worry about it. That's why we got a whole bucket. We'll get 'em later. Just keep standing in the box."

"Okay Coach." He turned around and stepped back up to the plate.

I grabbed another ball and threw it in. It sailed high over Noah's head. The next one was on the ground again, and the next one almost hit him. I bent down and picked up another ball. As I stood up, I saw Noah staring out at me with that same look behind his eyes that I had seen so often before.

"What?" I asked.

"Is this batting practice, Coach, or pitching practice?"

I had to laugh. "Oh, so you think you're real smart, do you? Okay, get ready. Here comes the heat."

I grabbed another ball, wound up, and threw it. It was right down the middle. Noah lifted his back elbow, stepped forward, and swung. I don't know if I heard the crack or saw it fly first, but I couldn't believe it. I spun on my heel and watched the ball sail into the outfield. When I turned back toward the plate, Noah was just standing there with the bat to his side and his mouth open.

"You smacked it, Noah! Run! RUN!"

Noah dropped the bat and took off toward first base. I kept yelling, "Go, Go, Go, Run!"

As he rounded second and headed for third, I jogged

toward home. When he came down the third base path, I was waiting. As he crossed home plate, I gave him a high five.

"You did it!" I yelled.

"I did it!" Noah yelled. "I smacked a homer!"

"I can't believe it. My first good pitch on our new field, and you hit it out of the park."

Noah was jumping up and down and dancing around.

"Okay," I said, "celebration's over. Let's pick up the balls and get back to practice."

We picked up the balls we had used, put them back in the bucket, and did another round of batting practice. Then Noah went out to second base, and I hit two buckets of grounders to him. After that, I hit a bucket of fly balls to center field.

I was getting worn out. So we put the balls back in the bucket, picked up the bat and gloves, and started walking back to the car.

"Coach?"

"Yeah."

"Can I take the bat home? I mean, just to show my mom?"

"Of course, Noah. It's yours."

"Really?"

"Yeah."

"Thanks."

"Coach?"

"Yeah."

"I really like our new baseball field."

"So do I."

Noah and I had been practicing on our field every day for a little more than a week—batting, grounders at second base, flies in the outfield. It became clear that his first hit that day had been a bit of beginner's luck. He needed some work at the plate. But he was slowly getting better at all aspects of the game. I wasn't the best coach. But that didn't matter. It was the practice that he needed.

The electronic tickets Noah and I had been waiting for had arrived on my phone app. When I'd gone to games with my dad as a kid, we'd bought paper tickets at the ballpark, and they weren't expensive. You could sit high behind home plate for three dollars.

But all that had changed. Not only had ticket prices skyrocketed, but ticket resellers had taken over the market and made it difficult to get tickets at their original price.

Luckily, I had a friend who worked for a company that held season tickets. That's what my earlier, annoying trip to the post office was about. I agreed to send him a 1958 excellent condition Mickey Mantle All Star Card for two season ticket seats to a Dodgers/Mets game. He had always admired the card, and I didn't really have any use for it anymore.

The seats were in the lower section behind the Dodger dugout. I told myself I was doing it for Noah. What an incredible way to see your first game. But I had to admit that I was pretty excited, too. I had never sat anywhere near that close before.

I picked Noah up late Sunday morning, and we headed out. We could have gone the same way that my dad and I used to. But a lot had changed with roads as well. So I took the 118 to the I-5 and then got off at Stadium Way. We parked and started walking to the ballpark.

"Can we get something to eat inside?" Noah asked.

I had to smile to myself. As another famous ball player, Yogi Berra, once said, "It's déjà vu all over again." But unlike my dad who was in the middle of his career, trying to support a growing family, I was retired with no one to worry about except myself.

"Sure," I said. We'll get hot dogs, peanuts, and maybe ice cream."

"Hey," I added, "Did you know that the first game I saw when I was about your age was the Dodgers and the Mets, just like this one?"

"Nope."

"And you know what happened?"

"Nope."

"Sandy Koufax, the pitcher for the Dodgers, threw a no-hitter!"

"Wow. Do you think that might happen today? I mean, a no hitter?"

"I wouldn't count on it. But maybe Trea Turner will hit a home run."

"Yeah. That would be great!"

As we walked into the stadium and turned down the aisle toward our seats, the field became visible for the first time. I had my eye on Noah.

"Wow," he said. "It's so huge. I didn't know it would be so huge."

"It's just like I told you. And look how perfect the diamond is, and how green the grass is."

"And how huge it is!" said Noah.

We made out way to our seats. They were so close it seemed like we could reach out and touch the players.

"Look," said Noah, "there's Trea out in the field. Number 6. He's right there!"

"Take a good look," I said. "And take a mental picture of what you see. You'll never see a major league field for the first time again."

"Why don't you just take a picture with your phone, Coach?"

I paused. There was no proper response to that. So I took out my phone and snapped a few pictures.

The Dodgers didn't win. They tied it up in the bottom of the ninth and sent it into extra innings. Then they lost five to four in the tenth. But it was a great game anyway.

When Trea Turner hit a home run in the first inning, I could barely keep Noah in his seat. After Turner rounded the bases, Noah turned and said,

"Hey Coach."

"Yeah?"

"Can I use your phone?"

"Of course."

I handed Noah the phone and watched as he dialed and waited for an answer.

"Hey Dad. Guess where I am!"

The next week was the last week of school. Noah and I continued practicing on our field through Wednesday. But I didn't see him on Thursday or Friday.

On Saturday morning, I had just fixed myself some coffee in the kitchen when I heard a noise in the backyard. I stepped into the dining room and looked out the window. Noah was standing in the middle of the rose garden with a shovel in his hands.

What?

I moved closer to the window. He was digging—wait, no!

"NO!" I screamed at the top of my lungs. Noah jerked his head toward the house. I slammed myself into the corner of the table as I ran to the door. I yanked it open and ran through the garage and out into the yard as fast as I could move.

"Stop it! Get out of there!" I yelled.

Noah dropped the shovel. He looked at me for a moment, frozen.

I stepped into the garden.

"Who told you, you could do that?"

I walked to the center of the garden, bent down, and picked up the red rose bush. In disbelief, I muttered to myself, "Look what you've done." I turned toward Noah, but he was already running around the corner of the garage.

I turned back and stared at the broken stem hanging from the packed dirt.

I saw Susan's hands as she gently pushed the soil around the roots while I held the bush in place.

Then I looked down into the hole.

I saw the thick, coiled ropes lowering the casket into the dark earth.

"No, no, NO!" I screamed, as I turned and hurled the bush as hard as I could against the side of the house.

I sank to my knees.

I don't know how long I was on my knees in the garden with tears rolling down my face. I stood up, picked up the shovel, and walked over to lean it up against the bench. And there it was. The new deep, red rose, sitting in a plastic can by the brick border.

Of course.

I went inside, grabbed my phone, and called.

Ashley picked up on the first ring.

"Hello."

"Hi Ashley. Is Noah there?"

"No. I thought he was with you. He was going to plant the rose. He was really excited. He made me drive him to the nursery yesterday. He bought it himself with the money he'd been saving. He isn't there?"

"No. I mean, yeah, he was. But he took off. I thought he ran home for a bit. It's nothing to worry about. I just thought he went home, but I think I know where he went. Don't worry. I'll call you back in a minute."

I hung up, jumped in the car, and drove to the church. As soon as I opened the door and got out, I could see Noah. I pulled my phone out of my pocket and called Ashley to let her know. Then I walked toward the backstop. Noah was sitting with his back up against it, his knees pulled up, and his face down.

"Hey Noah."

"Go away."

"Listen, buddy. I—"

"Just leave me alone."

I sat down beside him.

"No. I'm not going to leave you alone, because it was my fault. I shouldn't have yelled at you. I'm sorry."

"Then...why...did...you...do...it?" He was starting to cry and taking short breaths between his words.

"I don't have a good reason. That rose was just special to me."

"Why? What...do you...mean?"

I can't explain why. It just was. But you didn't know that, and I shouldn't have yelled at you."

"We dug out the other old roses."

"I know."

"I was trying to surprise you, like the baseball field. I was just trying to make the garden more beautiful."

"I know. I'm sorry. I'm really sorry."

I put my arm over his shoulders, and we sat there in the grass with our backs up against the backstop and the sun reflecting off the bases of the diamond.

PART VI

SPRING TRAINING

16

School was out and Summer League was starting in two weeks. Noah and I were practicing in the mornings since it was cooler. I usually drove to the church parking lot because I kept the bucket of baseballs in my trunk. Noah kept the bat with him. I almost never saw him without it. I think he slept with it.

Sometimes Noah would walk to the house and ride with me. I'd be sitting in the kitchen drinking a cup of coffee, and I'd see him coming down the sidewalk, T-shirt and tennis shoes, the bat over his shoulder with his glove hanging off the end. It was like a scene from a movie.

Other times I'd meet him at the field. On Friday, when I got to the parking lot and started walking toward the field with the bucket, I could see that Noah wasn't alone. There was another kid with him. He was shorter than Noah, with a slight build and sandy blond hair.

As soon as Noah saw me, they both started coming my way. The other kid was walking with a slight limp. We met between first and home. I set the bucket of balls down.

"Hi Coach. This is my friend Eric. I wanted to show him the field."

It took me by surprise. In all the time I'd spent with Noah, I hadn't ever thought about him having friends. I wasn't sure why. When I dropped him off at school that first day, he had walked straight in through the doors with his head down, not interacting with the other kids, and he had never mentioned a friend. Still, I felt kind of silly for not thinking about it before.

"Hi Eric," I said. "What do you think of the field?"

"It's great," Eric said. "I like the bases."

"They're Little League distance," Noah said.

I wasn't good at small talk with either adults or kids that I didn't know. So the best conversation starter for me was to get a game of catch going.

"Well, grab your mitts, and let's warm up. Form a triangle."

We started tossing the ball around. I threw it to Noah. Noah threw it to Eric. Eric back to me. It was clear that Eric had played before. He caught the ball with soft hands like someone who was used to catching and throwing. I was trying to think of a good opening question. After a couple of rounds, I asked,

"Are you guys in the same class at school?"

"Yup," Noah said. "Eric lives a couple of blocks over. His mom knows mine."

Eric thew one to me, dead center with a little snap to it.

"You sure know how to catch and throw, Eric. Are you in Summer League with Noah?"

"Nope," Eric said.

"He can't run," Noah said.

"Oh," I said, a little taken aback by Noah's bluntness.

My throw to Noah went wide. It bounced off his glove, and he had to turn and run after it.

"Yeah. My leg doesn't work right," Eric said.

"Did you hurt it," I asked.

"No. It's always been that way. I've had a couple of operations. I'm s'posed to have another one this summer."

"Does it hurt you?"

"Sometimes—a little. But I can't run, and my mom says I'm not s'posed to try cuz it can make it worse. But I like to watch baseball."

Noah had jogged back with the ball and tossed it to Eric.

"Yeah. Trea Turner is his favorite player, too. I told him about the game we went to and how Trea hit a home run in the first inning!"

"Yeah, Noah told me how huge the field was. He said you were sitting right behind the dugout."

"Do you think Eric could come with us to a game, Coach? That we could all go to a game like you and me did?"

Suddenly, I was trying to imagine what else I owned that I could trade to make that happen.

"Maybe. We'll have to see. I'm not sure."

I caught the ball from Eric and held on to it.

"Okay. Here's what we'll do. Eric, you play first base. Just stand with your left foot on the bag. I'll hit grounders to Noah at second, and he can throw them to you at first. Then you toss them back toward me at home. That way we can all practice, and Eric won't have to run."

We took our places. I grabbed a ball out of the bucket and hit a grounder to Noah's left. He scooted over, then sat back and stabbed at it with his mitt. It bounced over his glove and into right field.

"That's okay," I yelled, "You'll get the next one. Play the ball in front of you. Watch it into your glove."

I hit another one. Noah fielded it cleanly, took a shuffle step, and threw it to Eric at first. Eric caught it and threw it in my direction. The ball hit the ground and rolled toward the bucket.

"Perfect," I said.

"I like this," Eric said, "It's kinda like a real game."

"Okay, here comes another."

After a couple of bucket fulls, Noah went into the outfield to catch fly balls. Eric stood by me at home plate and picked up the balls that Noah threw back in. I couldn't help but see myself out there. There was nothing I loved more as a kid than chasing down fly balls. I would do it all day long if I could find someone who would hit them to me. I was tireless.

Eric reached into the bucket to hand me another one. But I stopped him. I waved to Noah.

"Okay guys, it's time to bring it in for the day." When Noah got to home plate, I added, "We'll do some batting practice tomorrow."

"Can we give Eric a ride home?" Noah asked.

"Sure."

We walked back to the car, put the bucket in the trunk, and climbed in.

"Seat belts on, guys?"

"Yup."

They fumbled with the belts until they clicked in place. I pulled up to the parking lot exit.

"You'll have to tell me where to go, Eric."

"Okay. Turn left here, and then right at the end of the street."

I followed Eric's directions. After several blocks, he said,

"You can drop me here. I live just down the street."

"I can take you to your house. It's no problem."

"Nah. Just drop me here."

I wasn't sure why it mattered, but I pulled over to the curb and let Eric out.

"Thanks for the ride."

"Okay. See ya later," I said.

"See ya," said Noah. Then he turned to me.

"Coach?"

"Yeah."

"Can Eric play with us again?"

"Sure. He seems like a nice kid."

"Yeah. We're friends."

I eased the car back into the street and drove to the house. I knew Noah would want to ride with me and then walk the couple of houses back to his place. When we pulled into the driveway, I turned to Noah.

"Your fielding was good today. You're improving everywhere, but especially with grounders."

"I missed a few, though. I have trouble with backhands."

"That's okay. Lots of people do. It's just a matter of practice and gaining confidence."

"What does that mean—gaining confidence?"

"It means feeling good about yourself, not worrying about how you play. The more you practice, the more certain you are that you can catch the ball, so you don't get nervous about it before it comes.

"But confidence isn't all about practice. It's also about having fun and playing for the love of the game. If you play because you love it, then you don't have to worry about what anyone else thinks who might be watching you. You just think about how good it feels to see that ball fly through the air, to run after it, and to watch it fall into your glove; or to scoop up that grounder and fire it to first. You're just having fun, and that's all there is to it."

"I do love playing. But I still get a little nervous sometimes."

"That's why we keep practicing. Just remember that it's about having fun and the love of the game. There's nothing else to worry about."

"Do you think I might be able to play second in Summer League?"

"I don't know. It depends on who else is playing and how good they are. And I guess it depends on the coach too. But you're chasing down fly balls pretty well too, so I'm sure you'll get to play somewhere."

"I hope my dad can come and see me play. He doesn't know how much better I've gotten from practice."

"Did he say he was coming this summer?"

"He said he might. It depends on his work."

"Well, we'll hope he gets to come. But if he doesn't, maybe we can take a video of one of your games."

"That would be great! Do you think we could?"

"Sure. It shouldn't be too hard. We could do it with my phone. But let's wait and see what happens."

17

We were gathered around the classroom waiting to go in for third period. I was nervous. I didn't know anyone. I had to do something. A group of guys were standing in a sort of circle. I walked over. There wasn't room to squeeze into the circle, so I stood behind, looking between two heads, trying to follow the conversation. Someone said something I couldn't hear, and they all started laughing. I laughed too. One of the guys turned and looked at me.

"What are you laughin' at?" he said.

The bell rang, and everyone headed for the door. I tagged along. As I slid down one of the aisles to find a seat, I heard someone say, "New kid's kinda goofy." I sat down and pulled out my book.

The teacher started talking. I tried to focus on the subject. But it was math class, something I knew I wouldn't have any trouble with. My trouble at the moment was figuring out how to fit in.

In the middle of my ninth grade year, the small private school I had been attending closed. So my parents enrolled me at a new, larger school. I didn't mind the idea of making new friends. I made friends easily given the right situation—one-on-one in known surroundings. But I was shy by nature, and being dropped into a new school by myself was like being parachuted behind enemy lines. It was frightening.

I scooted down the sidewalks with my head down, opened and closed my locker without looking too far left or right, and ate lunch by myself on a picnic table close to the parking lot. I managed to keep things together until the end of the day. But when my mom picked me up after school, I couldn't hold it in any longer.

"I hate it here, Mom." I said. "No one wants me here. I wanna go back to my old school."

"Well, sweetheart, you know you can't do that. It's only the first day. Things will get better. You just need to make some friends."

"No one wants to be friends with me. No one even talks to me."

"They don't know you yet, honey. Once they get to know you, you'll have lots of friends, just like your other school."

"No I won't," I replied. "I hate it."

After dinner, I asked my dad to play catch. We went out into the backyard. As we were warming up, he said,

"Your mom says your first day was a little tough."

"Why did you make me go there? I hate it. I'm lonely all day. I don't have any friends."

"You know the answer. There wasn't much choice. Your old school closed down."

My arm was getting warm and I was still angry. I threw one really fast.

"Hey," Dad said, "don't take it out on the ball!"

It made me laugh. My dad tossed the ball up in the air so I had to follow its flight back down into my glove.

"I know it's hard for you to remember," he said, "but there was a first day at your other school too."

"I guess." I threw it back, a little hard again.

"I'm serious. The first time at anything new is hard. Right now you love to play catch. It relaxes you. We play and talk at the same time. It's almost second nature. But there was a first time you tried to catch a ball that I threw you. It was hard for you. And a first time to try to catch a grounder. And a first time to try to hit a pitched ball with a bat."

"So?"

Dad caught the next one I tossed him and held onto it.

"The point is that every first is hard. But you stick with it. That's how you gain confidence. Right now it seems hard to make friends at a new place. You're not sure how. But you keep trying, and you will. It's a matter of time. Pretty soon you'll have lots of friends, and you won't even remember what that first day was like, just like you don't remember what your first baseball catch was like."

He threw a grounder to my right. I took a step and backhanded it.

"You caught that one like you've been doin' it all your life."

I smiled.

"Hey, baseball ought to be starting up at your school soon."

"Yeah, I saw a poster that said practices start tomorrow."

"You should sign up."

"I won't know anybody on the team. They probably won't want me there."

"Well, you need to sign up anyway because you can never be lonely while you're eating spaghetti."

"What?" I scrunched my face up. "What about spaghetti?"

"It's something someone said. 'No man is lonely while

eating spaghetti' because it takes too much concentration. Like this—"

He threw a hard grounder to my left. I took a couple of steps, caught it and tossed it back. Without missing a beat, he threw another to my right. I backhanded it and threw it back. Immediately back to my left. I returned it. Then to my right again. This time I caught and held on to it.

"Hey, what are you doin'?" I asked.

"Well, I think it's the same thing with grounders as it is with spaghetti. You weren't feeling lonely or worrying about your new school while you were catching those grounders, were you?"

"Nope."

"So sign up for baseball practice. That'll give you something to do at school every day that you love and that will take your mind off your worries."

The next day at school was more of the same—walking around by myself, wondering what the other kids were saying about me. I wasn't sure my dad was right. In fact, I was pretty sure he was wrong. But I did love baseball. So I brought my cap and glove and stashed them in my locker. When the closing bell rang, I grabbed my glove, put the cap on, and walked to the backstop in the field where the poster said to meet.

Standing there wasn't any different than waiting for class. The other kids all knew each other. They were talking and laughing, hitting each other in the shoulder. I wasn't feeling any better.

So I looked out across the diamond. It was really nice. It had a closely mowed grass infield with straight, brown base paths. The dirt part of the infield where the players stood was curved, wide, and raked smooth. The outfield even had fences so that you could hit an actual home run and not just have to leg it out.

When the coach showed up, I realized he was our science teacher. I liked that because he had called on me in class earlier, and I knew the answer. So I thought maybe he liked me. He told us that we were going to get into two groups. One group would take infield practice from him, while the other took outfield practice from his assistant. Then we would switch.

My group started with infield. The coach had someone play first base. Then one by one, we all rotated at shortstop. Coach would hit ten or twelve grounders. Then it was the next kid's turn. When I was up, I jogged out to my spot, crouched down, smacked my bare hand into my glove a couple of times, fixed my eyes on the coach, and waited.

I was anxious. Coach hit a hard grounder right at me. Instead of charging and short-hopping it. I sat back and let it bounce up into my stomach. It almost got away from me, but I managed to trap it and made a clean throw to first.

I can't explain what happened next. I squared up, got into position, bent my knees, and suddenly it washed over me—complete focus. I saw the coach getting ready to swing. I heard the crack of the bat as it hit the ball. There was nothing or nobody else that mattered, no other kids watching me, no comments to worry about, just me and the ball. I broke forward and left. It was so clear I could see the seams spin. I picked it up running and fired to first without breaking stride.

I was back in position in a moment. Crack—the coach hit it again. My eyes picked it up like slow motion. I stepped right, turned my glove early as I flung my left hand across my body, and watched the ball settle into the pocket. Then I slid to a stop, dug in my right foot and fired to first. To my left, to my right, slower, faster. It was an unbroken rhythm. I knew I wasn't going to miss. I was playing with confidence.

Then, whack—a line drive, hard to my right. I took two

strides and launched myself. I was horizontal with my left arm stretched as far as it would go. I felt the ball smack my mitt a second before I hit the ground. I stood up holding up my glove in the air to show I had the ball. Then I dusted myself off. As I walked off the field, I heard the coach say, "I think I've found me a ballplayer."

Outfield was next. As much as I wanted to play infield, I could get anxious about it. But outfield was a different matter. Outfield was my happy place. For me there was nothing like running across an expanse of green grass on a hot summer afternoon, gazing up at the spinning red seams of a white baseball as it cut its arc against a bright blue sky, timing my strides and the reach of my arm so perfectly that the ball dropped into my mitt like a plum ripe from a tree. I couldn't even begin to get nervous about outfield.

The coaching assistant hit a fly ball. I jogged over and caught it. He hit another a little harder. I sprinted so that I had time to stand there and wait while it fell down into my glove. I was moving left and right smoothly and quickly, making it look easy, almost daring him to challenge me. He kept hitting harder, and I kept pulling them in. I could tell he was enjoying himself. Each time, he'd yell, "Okay, how about this one."

Then he tagged one. It was deep and to my right. I took off at a dead run. I had my eye on it, but I could also see that I was getting close to the fence. I had to slow down. At the last second, I put on the brakes and jumped as high as I could. I snagged it just before it sailed over the top. I bounced up against the chain link but managed to keep my footing. When I looked back toward the coaching assistant, he had dropped his bat and was standing there laughing.

When practice was over and I was walking off the field, one of the other players caught up beside me and asked,

"Hey, did you play ball at your last school?"

"Yeah," I said.

Another kid walked up on my other side and said,

"That was a great catch you made against the fence. The coach couldn't stop laughing."

"Thanks."

"Hey, do you think Koufax will throw another no-hitter this year?" the first kid asked.

"I dunno. But I saw him throw his first one," I said.

"Really? Are you kidding?"

"Nope. My dad and I were at the game."

The three of us walked the rest of the way to the lockers, talking about Sandy Koufax and how many bases Maury Wills might steal this year.

18

On Saturday morning, I arrived at the field to another surprise. Not only were Noah and Eric there, but there were three other kids as well. They were all arguing.

"Hey," I said, "What's goin' on?"

"They say it's their field, Coach, cuz they were here first. I told 'em it belonged to us. We put the bases down."

Two of the kids looked older. One with long, straight brown hair said,

"We *were* here first. Fields don't belong to no one. They're just fields."

"It's ours," Noah said, "because we made it, we—"

"Okay," I said, "look, the field doesn't belong to any of us. It belongs to the church. I asked the pastor if we could play ball here, and he gave us permission. So we mowed the grass and put the bases in. But there's no reason that all of us can't play. It'll be more fun with more players. So let's get everyone's names."

"I'm Michael," the kid with the long brown hair said, "and that's Mateo." He pointed to the other older kid who had short black hair, brown eyes, and was wearing a Dodger cap.

"That's Jayden," Noah said, waving toward the kid who was about his size. "He's in my class at school."

I introduced Noah and Eric and then added, "While we're playing, you can all call me Coach."

"But we were playin' pickle. Now there's too many for that. But we don't have enough for two real teams," Michael said.

"That's okay," I said. "We'll play workup."

"What's that?" Noah asked.

"Everybody come in to home plate and I'll explain it."

I picked up the bucket of balls and walked toward the plate with all the kids following along. When I got there, I set the bucket down and said,

"Okay. Here's how it goes. I'll be the pitcher. We don't need a catcher because we have a bucket of balls. When we run out, we'll just stop and pick them all up again. Eric has a hurt leg, so he'll play first base. That leaves four of you.

"One of you will start as batter. One of you will play third, one shortstop, and the other outfield. Right field will be closed. That means that we draw an imaginary line from home plate right through second base on into the outfield. Anything hit to the right of that line is a foul ball.

"The batter gets just two outs. Then he goes out to the outfield. The outfielder goes to third base. Third base goes to shortstop, and shortstop becomes the batter. After we've rotated all around, we'll see who scored the most runs. I'll explain the rest as we play."

"Mateo. You be first up."

"Why does he get to bat first?" Noah asked. "It's really our field."

"It doesn't matter. Everyone gets a chance to play every position, including batting. That's why it's called 'workup.' You get to work your way through the positions until you get up to bat. Michael, take shortstop. Noah, take third. Jayden take the outfield, and let's play some ball."

None of us had warmed up, which went against my instincts. But trying to manage the new situation on the fly had already taken up a lot of time, so I didn't want to waste more. My first couple of pitches were off target. But the third one was right down the middle. Mateo smacked it hard, and it bounced between short and third and into left field. Jayden picked it up.

"Throw it in to second," Noah yelled.

Jayden threw the ball to Michael who was covering second base. Mateo had run to first base and stopped there.

"Good hit, Mateo." I said. Then I yelled loud enough for everyone to hear. "Now Mateo goes back to hitting, and we all remember there's an imaginary runner on first."

Then I turned to Michael and Noah and said, "So the play's at second if you get a grounder."

The next good pitch, Mateo hit a ground ball to Michael at short. He fielded it, ran to second, and stepped on the bag.

"Out!" I yelled. "That's one out."

Mateo had run to first and was standing there.

"Okay." I said, "Mateo, back to the batter's box. Imaginary runner on first again. Play's at second everyone!"

Mateo was a good hitter. I was throwing some pretty fat pitches up there, so I was a little worried that he was going to slam a comebacker right at me. I wasn't sure my reflexes were good enough to get out of the way in time if he did.

I bounced the next pitch on the ground. Then I thew one high that rolled up against the backstop. Finally, I put one in the strike zone. Mateo hit a high fly ball into short left field. Jayden had been playing in left center, so he had to run to his right and forward to get to the ball. Noah and I ran out toward him to see the play.

Jayden got there just as the ball was falling and stretched his arm out low and close to the grass. It looked like the ball hit the ground just in front of his glove and bounced in. Jayden swung his glove with the ball up into the air and shouted, "Caught it!" Then he started running in toward third base.

Noah glanced at me. His eyes met mine for a knowing second.

"Okay," I said, "that's two outs. Let's rotate positions."

Michael came up to bat. The others all moved up, except for Eric who stayed at first base. My first pitch to Michael was a good one that he swung on and missed.

"Keep your eye on it," I said. "Here comes another one."

The next pitch was good as well. Michael hit it straight to Noah at shortstop. Noah fielded it cleanly and fired to Eric at first. But his throw was a little to the home plate side of the bag. At the last moment, Eric stepped into the base path to catch it, and Michael, who was running full speed, crashed into him.

Eric yelled in pain as they both tumbled to the ground. I dropped my glove and ran toward first. When I got there, Michael was already up on his feet, but Eric was on the ground, crying and holding his leg.

"I'm sorry," Michael said. "I couldn't stop. I was going too fast."

"It's okay. It's not your fault," I said.

"Eric, is it your hurt leg?"

"Ye—yeah." He was crying, and it was hard for him to talk.

"It's gonna be okay. Just lie still. I'll take a look at it."

The kids had all crowded in around Eric.

"Are you okay?" one of the them asked.

"Yeah," said Noah. "Are you okay?"

"Hey," I said, "Everybody just back up a couple steps. Give him a little breathing room."

I looked at the leg that Eric had been holding. His jeans weren't torn, and there wasn't any blood anywhere.

"Eric, I'm going to press on your leg a little. Is that all right?"

"Okay."

I pressed gently up and down his leg.

"Does any of that hurt?"

"Nope." Eric had stopped crying and seemed to be calming down.

"Can you sit up?"

"I think so." Eric put his hands down on the ground and pushed himself slowly into a sitting position.

"Does anything hurt besides your leg?"

"Nope. I think I'm okay."

"We need to get you home. Okay, guys, game's over for today."

Everyone except for Noah took off. Eric was small for his age. So I picked him up and carried him to my car. Noah and I got Eric into the back seat, and Noah directed me to Eric's house.

At Eric's house, I knocked on the door and introduced myself to his mother. I told her what had happened. She came out to the car to help me get Eric into the house. On the way back to the house, she asked Eric,

"What were you doing playing baseball? You know you're not supposed to do that."

"Sorry, Mom."

"I thought you were just staying at Noah's house."

"But I wanted to play. Everyone else gets to—"

"You're not everyone else. You know you have to be more careful."

We had reached the door.

"Thanks for your help, Mr. Richards."

"Of course. I hope everything is okay, Eric. I'm sorry this happened, Mrs. Johnson."

"That's all right. You didn't know."

I got back in the car, and we started driving to my house.

"I noticed you didn't walk up to the house with Eric," I said to Noah.

"Yeah."

"It's like you didn't want to see his mom. Is that right?"

"I dunno."

"Did you know that Eric wasn't supposed to be playing baseball?"

"Yeah . . . But he really wanted to."

"So you and Eric told his mom that you were just going to hang out at your house?"

"Yeah."

"So you kind of lied to his mom."

"I guess so." Noah wrinkled his forehead and got the thoughtful look behind his eyes. "But it didn't happen like that, I mean, all at once. He just wanted to see the field. But then, you said he could play first base, and he really liked that. So then he wanted to come back. I didn't think it would matter."

I pulled into the church parking lot.

"Why are we here? I thought we were going back to your house?"

"I want to show you something."

We got out of the car and walked to the field. Then we sat down with our backs up against the backstop.

"Remember when we built the field?" I asked.

"Sure."

"Remember how we found the right place for second base?"

"Yeah. You told me to walk with the two pieces of twine in my hands until they were tight."

"Right. And I told you that math doesn't just describe what is beautiful. Math also tells us what is true."

"I remember. That was awesome."

"Yeah, it was, and it is. But it's not just awesome. It tells us that there's a relationship between what's beautiful and what's true—what's beautiful is often true, and what's true is often beautiful."

"Okay."

"For example, when we tell the truth to people, it helps them to have confidence in us, to trust us, which is beautiful. But when we tell lies, it stops them from trusting us; it makes the relationship less beautiful, like putting second base in the wrong place so it's no longer a diamond."

"I get it. I shouldn't have lied to Mrs. Johnson."

"That's right. And that's why truth is part of the Baseball Code."

"It is?"

"Yes. What are the parts of the code we've talked about so far?"

"Always work hard. Always do your best."

"And—."

"Always play fair. Always put the team first."

"Perfect. So the next parts are 'Always play with confidence. Tell the truth.'"

Noah nodded his head, but I could tell he was thinking. Not only did he have his serious look, he had a slight smile. He looked up at me and asked,

"So why didn't you tell the truth about Jayden not catching the fly ball when we were playing workup?"

"Yeah, I knew you saw that too. Here's the thing. Jayden said he caught it. If I said he didn't, I would've been calling him a liar."

"But you told me I was lying."

"True. But you and I are friends, and I talked to you in private to help you learn something important. If I had said that Jayden didn't catch the ball, I would've been calling him a liar in front of all the other kids and just embarrassing him."

"I guess. But Mateo wasn't really out."

"But we were playing a game. It didn't hurt Mateo to lose

one out at his time at bat. But it might have hurt Jayden a lot to be embarrassed in front of everyone. Remember, telling the truth is something to help make things beautiful. It's not a weapon to hurt people."

"Okay."

"So what are the new parts of the Baseball Code?"

"Always play with confidence. Tell the truth."

"Perfect. Okay, let's get going."

We started walking back to the car. When we got there, Noah turned to me and asked,

"Is that why the other parts say 'Always,' but the last part just says 'Tell the truth'?"

"That is a very good question."

PART VII

TRY OUTS

19

The Summer League Noah played in was held at a large park several miles from our neighborhood. It drew kids from a wide area. The park was a rectangle that had baseball diamonds at each corner. The diamonds were well-kept, but there wasn't any grass area on the infields. They were all raked dirt so that the bases could be moved to different lengths depending on the age of those playing.

The fields had no outfield fences. To hit a home run, you had to run all the way before the fielder could chase the ball down and get it back in. There were stands on each side of the backstop for family members and friends to sit in and watch the games.

It was a perfect Saturday morning. A strong wind the night before had pushed out any air pollution. The mountains that circled the Valley stood clear against the cloudless blue sky. The mood was festive. There were a couple of food trucks selling hotdogs, tacos, drinks, and various other snacks. Parents carried coolers with sandwiches for lunch. Younger brothers and sisters were running around.

Noah's mom had driven him to the field. She had to pay the

fees and sign the health and permission forms. I came later and sat down beside her in the stands.

"Hi Ashley. How's it goin'?"

"Hi Terry. Just signed everything. He's really excited. He's out there warming up."

She pointed toward the infield where kids were playing catch and throwing ground balls to each other.

I picked Noah out and watched him for a bit. I could tell he was nervous. He bobbled a couple of grounders that would be easy for him. I tried to catch his eye to reassure him, but he was all about business. Ashley noticed my attempts.

"I couldn't get him to look up here either," she said. "I really appreciate all the help you've given him with baseball—and with math. He's so excited about playing this year. Thanks. Really."

"I was happy to do it. It gave me an excuse to be around baseball again and even to play a little. I loved it when I was his age."

"I sure hope he does okay in the try-outs today."

"He'll be fine. But the try-outs aren't that important. What's more important is when he gets on a team and starts practicing."

The official information handed out said that try-outs were a way of trying to balance the teams. If coaches chose their teams individually or if the kids were assigned to teams randomly, then some teams might wind up with a lot of experienced players and other teams with none. Then games might be lopsided.

But with try-outs, the better players got spread around. The kids had numbers taped to their T-shirts. The coaches all watched them play—hitting, running, fielding. Then they sat down in private and chose their players.

Each coach, one after the other, made a first choice. Then each coach got a second choice, but this time they chose in reverse order. Then a third choice with the order of choosing reversed again. Then a fourth, and so on, until all the kids were on a team. Kids were never told when they were chosen. That way, all the teams had some experienced players and some less experienced so that the games were more competitive.

That was the theory.

The reality was a little less pure and a whole lot more chaotic. Noah had told me that most coaches had their own kids on their team. This made sense. Why else would a grown man give up Saturday mornings and a couple of evenings a week for practice during the summer? So it was an unwritten rule that coaches never picked another coach's kid.

The chaos came when try-outs started. Each kid was supposed to take some ground balls in the infield and some fly balls in the outfield. In the infield, the kids stood at shortstop. They were to field the ball and throw to first. But the coaches took turns hitting the ball, and some coaches were better at this than others.

The clearest example of the problem was what later became known as "Coach Stanmore's Battle with the Ball."

The kids all had their numbers taped to their T-shirts. But the coaches had T-shirts that had been printed up with their names on them—Coach Smith, Coach Ramirez, Coach Hunt, etc. They wore these throughout the season.

Kid number 65 was standing at shortstop waiting for his first grounder. Coach Stanmore, a slightly overweight, balding man, walked up to the plate and picked up the bat and ball. He tossed the ball into the air and swung. The ball dropped to the ground beside him. Most people were paying little attention, so there wasn't much reaction. He bent down and picked up the ball.

He tossed the ball again. But this time, he tossed it so far to his right that he didn't bother to swing. He just ran over, picked it up, and jogged quickly back to the plate.

His next toss was another swing and a miss.

Now the people in the stands were watching. They were silent, but one could feel it was a stifled silence that could erupt at any time.

This next toss was really high, and Stanmore swung so early that you could see air between the ball and the bat. That was the breaking point. Someone yelled,

"C'mon Stanny, you can do it!" A ripple of laughter broke across the crowd.

This infuriated Stanmore, who tossed it up again and swung with all his might—like Casey at the Bat. When he missed, his momentum spun him around almost a complete turn. He stepped backwards twice to catch himself. The crowd gasped in unison. Just when it looked like he was steadied, he lost his balance again and sat down in the dust. Mercifully, one of the other coaches came out to help him up and also took over the batting duty.

But Stanmore's battle was only an extreme instance of the wider problem. When Noah took the infield, the coach who was hitting swung and missed a couple of times before he tossed it up and connected with one. It dribbled out toward Noah's left. He ran forward, picked it up, and threw to first. The next one was so far to Noah's right that he had no chance of getting to it. The next one was a pop-up right at him that he caught easily.

"C'mon," someone yelled, "give him something to catch!" The crowd rumbled in support. Again, you had to feel a little sorry for the coach. He didn't have it in him. But he managed to hit a few more easy grounders, and Noah's turn was up.

The remaining try-outs were similar. Some kids got good balls to catch, others didn't. It was hard to judge how good the players were because the coaches' abilities were so uneven.

At lunchtime, the coaches gathered in the community room to make their choices. The parents and kids sat around at picnic tables or on the ground to eat lunch and wait for the rosters to be posted. I hadn't brought anything to eat. I was going to grab a taco from one of the trucks, but Ashley said that she had extra sandwiches.

We waited for Noah. Then we walked to her car, got the cooler, and looked for a place to sit. The picnic tables were all occupied. So we sat down under a tree, and Ashley passed around the sandwiches.

"I don't think I looked too good at infield today," Noah said.

"You did fine," Ashley said. "You didn't miss anything."

"But the coach hardly hit me anything. They didn't get to see that I can catch backhand."

"That's true," I said, "but the same thing was true for most of the kids. No one can tell much from the try-outs. Once you're on a team, you'll have a chance to show what you can do."

"Yeah, I guess," Noah said. Then he laughed. "I hope I'm not on Coach Stanmore's team."

"Now be nice," Ashley said.

"But Mom, he can't even hit the ball."

"That doesn't mean he can't be a good coach," Ashley said. "I mean, really, he might *know* a lot about baseball even if he can't play himself."

"Yeah, like how to fall on your butt."

"Okay, that's enough, Noah," Ashley said.

I jumped in to change the subject.

"You looked good in the outfield. You had a lot of hard fly balls hit to you, and you ran them all down."

"Yeah. But I really want to play infield this year."

"Well—"

"Hey, I think they've posted the teams. Everyone's goin' over there," said Noah.

He jumped up and took off running toward the Community Center. We both watched him disappear into the crowd of kids. Then Ashley turned to me.

"I apologize for what Noah said about Coach Stanmore."

"Oh, don't worry about it. It's typical kid stuff. Anyway, even though you do have to feel sorry for the guy, it was a little funny in its own way."

"That's true."

"It shows up the problem of finding people who are willing to coach. It's a big commitment of time, and not too many dads are willing to do it. That's why the coaches' kids are on their teams. It's not an ideal situation. But if it weren't allowed, there probably wouldn't be any coaches at all."

"I suppose so," Ashley said.

"Hey, do you mind if I ask something about Noah's dad?"

"No. Go ahead."

"The only reason I ask is because Noah brings it up from time to time. Is he coming out to see Noah this summer?"

"I don't really know. I mean, I really wish he would make a definite plan and stick to it. Noah really wants him to come. But I told him not to say anything to Noah unless it was certain this time because it's not fair to keep disappointing him."

"Okay. Thanks. I wanted to know the situation because Noah brings it up, and I didn't want to say the wrong thing and get his hopes up if there weren't plans or anything. So nothing is certain at this point?"

"Right."

Noah came walking back toward us. He sat down with a glum look on his face.

"What's up?" I asked.

"I'm on Coach Tasker's team."

"What's wrong with that?"

"His son's on the team—Danny. He's in my class at school. I don't like him at all. He's kind of a bully. He makes fun of Eric."

"But do you know Coach Tasker?"

"No."

"So Danny is just one kid on the team. Coach Tasker might be a great coach for all you know. Besides, your job isn't to worry about the coach, your job is to work hard, and—"

"Do my best."

Noah repeated the right words, but the music wasn't in them.

20

Susan and I were sitting in the living room of our tiny one-bedroom apartment. It had been about a month since we returned from our honeymoon. We were both back in school. Susan was working on her bachelor's in literature, and I was in a master's program in mathematics. Evenings were always study time. Susan looked up from her book and said,

"I think marriages should be five-year contracts."

"What?"

"You know, rather than 'till death do us part,' it should be a five-year contract."

"Are you trying to tell me something?"

Susan started laughing. She rocked her head and shoulders slightly back and around.

"No. I'm perfectly happy, of course."

"Then what are you talking about?"

"I'm saying that a lot of marriages don't work out. Over time, the people realize they don't get along as well as they thought. So promising to stay together forever doesn't make sense. How do you know how you'll feel about the other person thirty years from now? Maybe you should just try it out—a five-year contract."

"Where is this coming from? Is this something you're talking about in a lit class?"

Susan loved philosophical discussions. A lot of them had their roots in literature that she read in her classes. My studies didn't lend themselves quite as easily to lively conversation— What are your thoughts on Goldbach's conjecture?

"In part, yes," she said, "I've been reading Thomas Hardy's *Jude the Obscure*. He suggests that it's kind of silly for two people to stand in front of a minister and promise to feel the same way about each other for the rest of their lives as they happen to have felt for the last little while."

"That makes sense. But, as I recall, you're the one who once argued that love is more about how we choose to act and not so much about how we happen to feel."

"Yeah, that's true." Susan thought about it for a while. "But you can't control how the other person chooses to act. What if you married someone who turned out to be an axe murderer?"

I laughed. "Well, there are always extremes and exceptions. I mean, you've got to walk away from the axe murderer. But that's not the same as replacing traditional marriage vows with five-year contracts."

"Oh, I'm just teasing about that—although I do think that some people would be better off with a five-year contract, I mean, if they're not serious. But I like the traditional vows, that's why I said them. I think Hardy was on to something, though. There's a question about what we can and cannot promise."

"Like what?"

"Well, Hardy saw promising to love someone forever as about romance, about promising to feel 'in love' forever. So he thought that it was silly."

"Okay."

"And, of course, he was right that a lot of people—especially young people—who get married and make that promise probably do look at it that way."

"But others, like you and me, for example, don't," I said. "We see it as promising to act a certain way."

"Sure. But even so, I don't know what the future will bring, so can I really make that promise?"

"Why not? If we're not talking about feelings any more, but we're talking about actions, you're in charge of your own actions."

"I'm not so sure," Susan said. "What if I promised to take care of you forever, and then I got in an accident that incapacitated me or even just lost my job? I wouldn't be able to keep my promise."

"But that wouldn't be your fault."

"I'm not talking about whose fault it would be. I'm saying that since we can't control everything about the future, we can't make promises about things we can't control."

"Okay," I said, "but marriage vows aren't promises to 'take care of each other.' They are promises to 'love each other.'"

"I agree," Susan said. Her blue eyes were sparkling above the freckles across her nose. "But that's why Hardy is helpful. He asks us to question what we can promise and what we can't. We can't promise how we will feel in the future, and we can't promise everything about our future actions either."

"So what are we promising?" I asked.

"I think when we promise to love someone 'till death do us part' we're saying, 'I'm going to try to do what's good for you. I'm not sure I can, but I'm willing to try. I won't ever give up. I'm going to do my best.'"

21

I walked to the parking lot with Noah and his mom. We got in our respective cars, and I headed home. I knew that Noah wasn't happy with the outcome of try-outs. It was one of those times when grown-ups and kids saw things through different lenses. Noah was young enough that each day's events, no matter how significant, filled his field of vision. They either lifted him to the height of exuberance or dropped him into the depth of despair. I was at the other end of life. Sure, there were momentous events that changed things forever. But, for the most part, each day was a drop in a flow with gradual and cumulative effect.

I pulled into the garage, got out, and went into the house. I poured a glass of water at the sink and sat down at the dining room table, looking out into the backyard. The afternoon had gotten quite warm. I had intended to do a little reading. But I realized that I should probably put a little extra water on the roses. So I dropped the glass in the sink, walked through the garage, picked up the hose, and turned on the spigot.

I walked around the brick border, trying to spray the water close to the base of the plants rather than on the leaves or blooms. As I was working around the back side, the hose caught. I gave it a jerk, and I heard something fall. I walked back to the side and saw that I had knocked over the plastic can with the new rose that Noah had brought over a couple of weeks ago. I had left it sitting there by the side of the garden. I kept it watered, and it was doing okay. But I wasn't going to be able to leave it in the can forever.

I finished up, went back inside, and sat down to read. . . .

Susan and I were sitting on the bench in the late afternoon. It was the golden hour. Soft, warm light was falling across the colors of the garden. Susan turned to me and said,

"I think we need to replace the rose bush in the center. It doesn't look very good anymore."

"You mean the first one we planted together?"

"Yes."

"But that's where the whole thing started."

"I know. But it's not doing well. Some plants don't last as long as others."

"That's true. But maybe we should give it a little more time."

"The point of the garden is its beauty. Our job isn't to decide which plants last the longest. Our job is to keep the garden blooming."

"What did you say?"

I turned. Something wasn't right. Everything was fading. I tried to hang on. I yelled, "WHAT?"

My own voice startled me. My eyes opened and focused on the Renoir across the room. I turned to look at the clock on the table next to me. It was 7:10 p.m.

～

On Monday morning, I picked up Eric and Noah and drove to our field. Since his fall, Eric had kept coming to the field with Noah and me to practice. It turned out that the accident didn't do any serious damage to his leg. His mom was upset that he and Noah had misled her, but she also realized how much he loved to play. So she made me promise her that I'd put him where he wouldn't have to run and where no one would run into him.

If Mateo, Michael, and Jayden all showed up, we played workup with Eric on first base. But we used imaginary runners all the time rather than having the batter run to first. If the infielder caught the grounder and threw it to Eric at first, and he caught it, then the imaginary runner was out. But if the infielder bobbled the ball or if Eric dropped the throw, then the imaginary runner was safe. It was that simple.

If only one or two of them came, we sometimes played five hundred. Or I might hit grounders and flies to them and then throw some batting practice, like I would if it were just Noah, Eric, and me.

This morning, when we arrived, no one else was there. We formed the usual triangle and started warming up. I tossed the ball to Noah, and asked,

"So when's your first practice?"

"Tomorrow night."

"That's great. You'll get to meet the coach and show him what you can do."

Eric threw the ball wide to my left. I had to take a step to reach it.

"Sorry, Coach," said Eric. "Whose team are you on, Noah?"

"Coach Tasker's," Noah said.

"Well, you're not gonna play shortstop, that's for sure," Eric said. "Danny will get to play short. He's such a jerk. He always calls me names."

I caught the throw from Eric and held on to it.

"Listen, guys, let's not borrow trouble."

"Borrow what?" Noah said.

"Borrow trouble."

"What does that mean?" Noah asked.

"It means let's not worry about problems before they even happen. Sure, we all know that coaches favor their own kids. That wouldn't change no matter which team you were on. But you don't want to play shortstop anyway, Noah. You'd like to play second. So let's wait and see what happens."

"Okay, Coach." They both acquiesced in unison.

We threw the ball around the triangle a few more times, and then Eric took first, Noah went into the outfield, and I carried the bucket of baseballs to home plate to hit some flies. I picked up the first ball, tossed it up, swung and missed completely.

"Hey!" Noah yelled.

I knew what was coming.

"Hey, Coach Stanmore!"

"Yeah. You can do it, Stanny!" Eric yelled.

Noah had clearly shared the now famous story with his friend. They were so delighted with themselves. Noah was rolling on his back in left field, and Eric was laughing so hard he had to sit down on first base. There was nothing for me to do but stand there while they laughed it out.

After we finished practice, on our way back to the car, Noah asked,

"Eric, when is your operation?"

"My mom said about a month, I think."

"Are you worried about it," I asked.

"No. I've had 'em before. I'm used to it."

"Does it hurt?" Noah asked.

"A little, afterwards. It's not too bad. But I won't be able to play baseball for a while."

"We'll come and visit you," Noah said.

"We sure will," I said.

We arrived at the car and piled in.

"Seatbelts on?" I asked.

"Yup."

We dropped Eric off and then headed to my house. When we pulled into the garage, I said to Noah,

"Hey. Can you help me with something?"

"Sure, Coach."

I grabbed two pairs of garden gloves and handed one to Noah. Then I picked up the pruning shears and the shovel and headed out the back door. Noah followed. When we got to the garden, I pointed to the rose sitting by the brick border in the plastic can.

"This has been sitting here since the day you brought it. I think it's about time we planted it, don't you?"

"Sure."

I bent down, took the pruning shears, and cut the plastic can away from the roots. Then I picked the bush up and said,

"Would you grab the shovel."

Noah picked up the shovel, and we walked to the center of the garden.

"Now dig the hole a little deeper, and pull out any old roots that you see."

Noah started digging slowly and carefully. He bent down from time to time and pulled out the old roots.

"Okay. That looks good," I said.

I bent down and placed the new bush in the hole. It still wasn't quite deep enough. So I lifted it out and set it down. Then I dug a little more dirt out with my hands. This time when I set the bush in, it was perfect.

"You know what," I said to Noah, "I forgot the potting soil.

Can you run into the garage and grab the bag. It's under the work bench. It's yellow."

"Yup."

As I waited for Noah, I looked out from the center of the garden at the bench. It was old now, a little rusty here and there. I couldn't help recalling when it was new. We had placed it there shortly after we first finished the garden.

"Here it is, Coach." Noah was holding the bag beside me.

"Okay. While I hold the bush in place, you shake some soil from the bag around the edges to fill in the gap. Mound it up a little so you can push it in later."

I set the bush in the center. Noah poured the potting soil around the perimeter.

"Now. Set the bag down, and push the soil in with your fingers."

Noah started to push the soil into the gaps around the bush. But I stopped him.

"No. Wait a minute. Let me do it. You hold it in place."

While Noah held the rose, I took my gloves off and pushed the soil down into the gaps. The soil felt cool and good against my fingers. I worked around the plant until it was all filled in, smooth and even on the top.

"I like planting things," Noah said.

"So do I."

I sat back and looked across the rest of the garden. I could feel that the new rose belonged there—that it was right.

"Coach?"

"Yeah."

"What are you doing?"

"I was just thinking."

"What?"

"That it's funny how we can describe what is beautiful. But we don't have to describe it to feel it, to enjoy it. It's the same with truth. We can describe it. But we don't have to describe it to feel it, to know it."

"What does that mean?"

I looked at Noah with his dark brown hair falling across his forehead and his thoughtful eyes, and I said,

"It means . . . thanks for the rose."

PART VIII

CLOSE CALL

22

I picked up Noah and Eric and headed toward the park for Noah's second game. Ashley wasn't going to make it. She had been called in to work.

Last week was the first game, and it had gone well. Noah's team didn't win, but they only lost by one run, and Noah got a hit. Noah liked his coach more than he thought he would. Of course, the coach's son, Danny, did get to play shortstop, just as everyone expected. Noah didn't even get to play second base. He was in left field. But he was going to get a chance.

The kid playing second was older than Noah. So he was faster and had a stronger arm. But his family was moving in the middle of the season. Coach Tasker told Noah and Matt, another kid who was interested, that they could compete for the position. He would decide based on how well they did in practice and games and the level of commitment they showed the team.

We pulled into the lot and parked.

"Okay, guys, here we are. Got your glove, Noah?"

"Yup."

"Can you grab the water bottles, Eric?"

"Sure."

We hopped out of the car. Noah took off running and yelled over his shoulder to us,

"See ya after the game."

"Okay. Play with confidence!" I yelled back.

Eric and I walked to the stands and found a place to sit.

"I wish I could play first base out there like I do on our field," Eric said.

"Yeah, that would be cool."

"But they don't use imaginary runners like we do."

"That's true, although imaginary runners might be helpful to them at times."

Eric laughed. "Yeah, no kidding."

Eric loved the game. It was hard to see him having to sit and watch when he wanted to play so badly. But he was good about it, and it helped a lot that he got to play with us on our field.

"Do you think you might be able to play more after your next operation?"

"My mom says maybe. We have to wait and see."

"Okay, here we go."

The umpire had called "Play ball!" and the game was underway.

Summer League for ten to twelve-year-olds isn't like the Little League World Series. There aren't a lot of extra-base hits or home runs. Most kids get on base by fielding errors or walks. But there's still a lot of running, throwing, cheering, and general excitement from all the parents watching the game.

Noah was first up in the top of the second inning.

"C'mon, Noah," Eric shouted, "knock one out there."

"Eyes on the ball, Noah," I yelled.

Noah watched the first pitch sail by. It was right down the middle—strike one.

"That's okay Noah." I called out, "You've got the next one."

The next pitch was high and tight. Noah leaned back and

watched it go by. He stepped out of the batter's box, took a couple of swings, and stepped back in.

The next one was a little high and outside. Noah took a strong cut anyway. He was behind the ball, but he made contact and sent it on a line over the first baseman's head. Eric and I jumped to our feet and started yelling.

"All right, Noah. Go! Run, run, run!"

Noah rounded first and started toward second, but the right fielder scooped up the ball and got it back in. So Noah trotted back to first.

"Okay, Noah. Way to hit!" I yelled.

I could tell Noah was excited to be on base. But his excitement was short-lived. The next batter hit a ground ball to the shortstop who threw Noah out at second base. But that was only the first out. The team managed to get a run before the inning was over even though they left a couple on the bases.

In the field, Noah was doing well. He caught a fly ball, and he didn't let anything on the ground get by him.

The top of the third turned out to be a big inning for Noah's team. When Noah came up there were already runners on first and second with only one out. The first pitch was waist high. Noah swung and missed. "Wow," I thought to myself. "I wish he'd hit that one. He was dialed in."

"C'mon, Noah. Knock it outta the park," yelled Eric.

The next pitch was low and outside, almost in the dirt. The catcher couldn't trap it, and it scooted through to the backstop. The runners took off. By the time the catcher corralled the ball, both runners had advanced. The catcher just tossed it back to the pitcher.

The next pitch was way inside. Noah tried to jump back, but it caught him good in the left arm. You could hear the pop. A muffled gasp went up from the stands, and I instinctively stood to my feet. But Noah had already dropped his bat and was jogging toward first base, rubbing his arm.

Batters hit by pitches were pretty common in Summer League. It's not that batters tried to get hit or didn't have quick reflexes. But young pitchers were still struggling to learn control, and their pitches were often more than a little inside. Thankfully, the kids wore helmets, and most of the pitchers didn't throw that hard.

The inning ended with Noah's team scoring four runs. Because they had batted around the lineup, Noah would probably have come up again in the top of the fourth. But in the bottom of the third, something happened that changed that.

The opposing team had scored three runs. They had a runner on third with two outs. It was now five to four in favor of Noah's team. With the count at two and two, the batter hit a deep fly into left center. Noah took off running back and toward his left. The base umpire ran out a few steps to watch the catch.

Noah was flying. Without breaking stride, he stretched his glove out and down toward his front foot. Noah's glove, his foot, the ball, and the grass all seemed to come together for an instant. Then he slammed on the brakes and slid to a stop.

The umpire hesitated before making the call. The sun was shining in toward the field, making it hard to see. It looked like he was just starting to raise his right fist to signal an out when Noah turned back toward the infield and shook his head. Rather than swinging his glove up high to show "I got it," he picked the ball out of his glove and threw it in to the shortstop. The umpire gave the "no catch" sign. The runner from third had already tagged up and scored, and the batter was standing on second with a double.

I settled back down into my seat.

"That's too bad," I said to Eric. "I thought he had it."

"Yeah, me too."

I grabbed my bottle of water and took a couple of swallows. Then I looked up and saw Coach Tasker waving at Noah. Noah came jogging off the field and sat down on the bench. The coach talked to him for a few moments. Then he turned to another kid who grabbed his glove and ran out to left field.

I wonder if Noah hurt himself?

"I'll be right back," I said to Eric. I stood up, climbed down the rungs of the bleacher, and walked over behind the bench area where Noah was sitting. I leaned with my hands against the chain link that separated the fans from the team.

"Hey, Noah," I said, "are you okay?"

"Yeah. I'm fine."

"Why'd the coach take you out?"

"I dunno."

"You dunno? The coach didn't say anything?"

"Yeah, maybe. It's okay. I'm fine."

That's when it hit me. I knew exactly what was going on. I couldn't believe it. I turned and walked down toward the other end of the bench where Coach Tasker was standing.

"Hey, Coach Tasker, why'd you pull Noah out of the game?"

"Huh?" Tasker turned around to see me standing on the other side of the fence.

"I said, why'd you pull Noah out of the game?"

"It was time for someone else to play."

"Really? In a close game like this? He played the whole game last week. He's one of your best players."

"Yeah, well, he needed some time to think."

"To think about what?"

"To think about the team."

"Yeah. There it is. You're mad because he didn't lie about catching the ball. That's just great."

"Hey, it's the umpire's job to call the plays. Not his. He needs to understand that. He might've cost us the game."

"Perfect. You wanna teach the kids that they should win by cheating. That's a great example."

"Hey, go sit down. Get outta my face."

"I'd be happy to."

I kicked the bottom of the chain link fence hard enough to hurt my foot. Then I climbed back up to my seat.

"What were you talkin' to Coach Tasker about?" Eric asked.

"Nothing really. He can be a little difficult."

"He's probably just like his son."

23

The boys' locker room in my high school was in the basement, underneath the new classroom and music building that was built my sophomore year. When you went down the stairs and walked toward the lockers, the coaches' office was on the left. We went past it at least twice a day, coming and going from baseball practice.

By the door was a big window. There was no curtain or anything, so you could always see in. Sometimes our coach would be there, sitting at the desk, or sometimes the head of the P.E. Department. But most of the time the office was empty. There wasn't much there—a desk, the coaches' jackets and shoes, notebooks and schedules, old pieces of equipment.

But on a small table up against the window was a stack of new baseballs. These were the official Spalding balls that came in bright red, white, and blue cardboard boxes. The coach kept these for games.

On Thursday, I came in early from practice. I had twisted my right ankle a little. Coach said I should get off it and then tape it up for tomorrow's game. I walked down the stairs. As I passed the office, I looked to my left almost by habit. Jim

Freeman was standing in the office by the window. He had a brand new baseball in his hand, and he was putting the empty box back in the stack. He looked up and saw me. Then he put the ball in his pocket and walked toward the door.

Jim was the star pitcher on our team. He was a senior, six foot two, and totally full of himself. Even though I was one of the better players on the team, he never gave me the time of day because I was a sophomore and not cool enough. When he came out the office door, I was already several steps past.

"Hey Richards," he said.

I turned around.

"Nobody cares about a few missing baseballs, as long as everyone keeps their mouths shut. Got it?"

I lifted my chin in acknowledgment, turned, and walked on.

After dinner that night, I didn't ask my dad to play catch. I went straight to my room to do homework. Usually, if something was bothering me, catch was the time to talk it over. But I knew talking it over with my dad wouldn't help because I already knew what I should do. I should tell Coach what I saw, tell him that Jim stole one of the new game balls.

But I didn't want to. I didn't like Jim at all, and I didn't care if he got in trouble. In fact, I'd have been happy if he got in trouble for what he did. But Jim was a senior. He was a star on the team, and he had lots of friends. He knew I was the one who saw him take the ball. So if I told, he would know it was me, and he would make it hard on me with the team.

I wished I hadn't left practice early. I wished I had walked past the office without looking in the window. I wished I'd never seen anything. I kept worrying about what to do until I wore myself out and fell asleep.

The next day, after our game, Coach came into the locker room while we were changing.

"Listen up," he said. "A couple of new game balls have gone missing from the office. I never thought I'd have to do this here, but I'm gonna start locking them up in the cupboard.

"Now I'm not saying it was someone on the team. In fact, I'd really hate to think it was. But if one of you took the balls or if one of you knows something about it, I expect to hear from you in my office by Monday. Okay? That's it."

I couldn't help but look over at Jim. He was making sure not to look at me. I finished dressing. Then I grabbed my glove and headed out. When I was walking up the stairs, someone elbowed me hard and knocked me against the wall as he walked quickly past me. I regained my balance and looked. It was Jim.

After practice on Monday, I dressed and walked past the coaches' office. Coach was in there, sitting at his desk. I'd been thinking about little else all weekend, trying to decide what to do. As I looked in the window, Coach looked up and caught my eye. It wasn't until that very moment that I made up my mind.

I waved and kept walking.

As I climbed up the stairs, I said to myself, "It's only a couple of baseballs. No one on the team will remember it. The coach will forget about it. I'll forget about it."

I didn't.

24

After I took Eric and Noah home from the game, I drove to the church parking lot and pulled in. I wasn't going to the field. I was dropping in on Pastor Thompson unannounced. I was hoping he was in his office on a Saturday afternoon because I was still fuming over what had happened to Noah. I was mad at Coach Tasker for being such a jerk. And, to be honest, I was mad with myself for sticking my nose in it because I knew that probably hadn't made things any better for Noah.

Thankfully, Pastor Thompson was there. He saw me coming and waved me into his office like he had on my previous visit. I wasn't sure exactly what it was. But just the sight of his smile and his relaxed frame leaning back in the chair lowered my blood pressure. I walked into the office.

"Hey TR, how are ya? Have a seat."

"Hello Pastor John, I'm doin' okay." I settled into a chair in front of the desk and crossed my legs.

"I'd guess that's not entirely true or you wouldn't be here," said Pastor Thompson. "I haven't seen you in weeks, not since we talked about the field, although I've seen you out there playing with Noah and the other kids."

"Oh, yeah. Thanks again for letting us use the field. It's been a great place to practice."

"So what can I do for you this afternoon, TR?"

"Well, it's kind of about Noah."

"How so?" Pastor Thompson put his hands behind his head and leaned back further in his chair.

"I've been helping Noah with baseball and with his math homework."

"I know. Ashley told me. That's been good for him. She really appreciates it."

"I've also been talking with Noah about working hard and playing fair, you know, doing the right thing."

"Okay."

"Well, this morning, he had a baseball game in Summer League. He was playing left field, and a fly ball was hit to deep left center. Noah took off after it. He tried to make a shoestring catch with his mitt down close to the grass. The umpire couldn't see well because of the sun and the angle of the play. So the ump was just about to signal a catch when Noah shook his head, and the ump ruled 'no catch' instead.

"That was fine. But then Noah's coach benched him for telling the truth. He told Noah that he should have pretended that he caught the ball and let the umpire go ahead and make the wrong call. He said Noah let the team down.

"I was so mad. I told the coach what I thought right then and there. How does he get off teaching kids to cheat? So now, not only is the coach mad at Noah for telling the truth, he's probably even more mad because I called him out. And that's my fault. I should've controlled my temper."

Pastor Thompson leaned forward and put his elbows on the desk.

"So," he said, "what are you here for, absolution?"

I didn't respond immediately. Pastor Thompson kept looking at me.

"Oh, I don't know. I don't know why I'm here. I didn't know where else to go. I'm just still angry about the whole thing."

"Well, I'm not sure I know the answer to your problem. But I'm pretty certain that being angry isn't it."

"Yeah, I know."

"So maybe you give it some time. Sleep on it. It probably won't seem so serious in the morning. The coach might forget the whole thing before you do. He has to deal with all kinds of issues with players, parents, and overzealous fans."

I took a deep breath and exhaled slowly. Then I sat there silently for a few moments.

"That's the right advice, in general, I know. But there's something else I haven't told you."

Pastor Thompson smiled. "You didn't hit him, did you?"

"No," I chuckled, "but I sure felt like it. I did kick the fence pretty hard. No, what I left out is that Noah and another kid are in a competition to play second base for the team. So now I'm afraid that the coach will hold what I did against Noah."

"Did he suggest something like that?"

"No."

"Well, then why do you think that? That would be an unusually mean-spirited thing to do to a kid."

"I know. But I don't trust him—someone who would punish a kid for being honest."

"I think you might be going out of your way to borrow trouble."

I shifted in my chair.

"It's funny that you say that."

"Why?"

"I don't know. It's just something I've heard lately."

"Why don't you talk to Noah's coach?"

"Talk to him? I don't even know him, and I'm sure I'm the last person he wants to hear from.'"

"That may or may not be true. But you said you're afraid what you did will affect Noah, right?"

"Right."

"And you feel responsible—that you should have controlled your temper. So why not take the responsibility to try to fix things? I don't see how it could make things worse."

I sat quietly for a while. Silences never seemed to bother Pastor Thompson. They were like part of the conversation.

"You know I didn't really come here to get an assignment."

Pastor Thompson smiled. "I'm sure you didn't."

I pushed myself up out of the chair.

"Okay, John, I'll give it some thought."

"Take care of yourself, TR."

Pastor Thompson walked out from behind the desk, stuck out his right hand to shake mine, and put his left hand on my shoulder.

"I mean that," he said, looking right at me, "and don't be a stranger."

"Thanks."

I walked out, got in my car, and started thinking about the best way to get Coach Tasker's number.

Sunday afternoon, I backed my car out of the garage and headed to the coffee shop on the corner by Jake's Grocery. Pastor Thompson was right. I knew I'd made things worse, and I had to try to patch it up for Noah's sake. I didn't want to talk to Coach Tasker at all. But if I was going to talk to him, it wasn't going to be on the phone. It had to be face to face. So I had called and set up a meeting.

I parked the car and walked in through the front doors. The young woman behind the cash register asked,

"Will there be just one this afternoon?"

"Actually, I'm meeting someone," I said. I looked to my left, and right away saw Coach Tasker sitting at a booth by the window. I turned back toward the woman.

"There he is," I said.

I walked over to the booth.

"Mind if I join you, Coach Tasker?"

"Of course, Mr. Richards. Grab a seat. It's Bob, by the way."

"Thanks. And it's Terry."

I reached out my hand. We shook politely as I scooted into the booth.

The server came over and brought us both coffee. She asked if we wanted anything else. I was ready to say no, when Bob broke in and said that I couldn't leave without trying their raspberry pie. I acquiesced, and she left with our order.

I took a sip of coffee.

"Bob, the first thing I want to do is apologize. I shouldn't have hassled you in public yesterday about taking Noah out of the game. I was out of line, and I'm sorry."

"Thanks. I appreciate that. Don't fret about it. Things like that happen in the heat of the moment. By the way, are you Noah's grandpa? I've only met his mother. Your last name's not the same."

"No. I'm just a friend. I've been helping him with baseball."

"Well, it's workin'. He knows the game."

"Look, Bob, I meant it when I said I was sorry for yelling at you on the field, you know, in public. I should've set up a time in private like this to talk about it. But I don't think what I said was wrong. I still think it was wrong to bench Noah for telling the truth."

"Well, now, you know I can't agree with that. It's the umpire's job to make calls, not the player's. That's something all the kids need to understand."

The server came back and set the raspberry pie down in front of us. We both took a couple of bites.

"You were right, Bob. That's pretty good pie."

"I'd never lead ya astray."

"I agree that the ump has to make the calls behind the plate for balls and strikes because he's the one in the right position to do so. I also agree that he has to make the calls for plays at the bases, not only because he's usually in the position to have the best view, but also because players from both teams are involved, and their views are biased.

"But with a fly in the outfield, like the one with Noah, the umpire wasn't in a position to see the play. Noah was the only one who knew whether he caught the ball or not. He was obviously telling the truth because he said he *didn't* catch it. If we tell him to let the umpire call it a catch, then we're telling him to be dishonest. Why would we do that?"

"We do that because the idea is to win. If the umpire calls it a catch, that's a lucky break for the team. Noah shouldn't have thrown away a lucky break for the whole team."

"But it wasn't a 'lucky break.' It was a missed call. How would you feel if you were on the other side? Would you want your team to lose because the umpire missed the call?"

"Hey, stuff happens, my friend, stuff happens. Ya live with it."

"But aren't we supposed to be teaching the kids to play fair and to be honest?"

"It ain't about bein' honest. It's about lettin' the ump do his job and you doin' yours."

I took another bite of raspberry pie, and washed it down with a gulp of coffee.

"Okay. Well, we're clearly going to disagree about this. But I know that Noah is competing with Matt to play second base, and I'm hoping our disagreement won't be held against him."

Bob had just put a bite of pie in his mouth. He dropped the fork back on his plate with some force.

"Now that ruffles my feathers a bit. What would make you say such a thing?"

"I was just worried, I mean, I yelled at you at the field, and I thought it might affect the way you viewed Noah."

"Of course, I wasn't happy with your yellin' at me at the field. Would you be? But you apologized, and I said not to fret about it, and I meant it. Look, we disagree about some things. But I would never take it out on the kids. Why do you think I'm out there every Tuesday and Thursday night and every Saturday if it's not for them? I like Noah. He and Matt'll battle it out. I'll call 'em as I see 'em, and I'll treat 'em fair."

"Thanks. I appreciate that."

"I think you fret too much over nothin'."

"Yeah, somebody else told me something similar recently."

"Oh yeah. Who?"

"It's not important. I just wanted to make sure things were right between us."

"Right as rain."

On Monday morning, all the kids showed up at the field. So we played workup, and then I threw batting practice for everyone for a while. Noah seemed a little lackluster. I knew we were going to have to talk about Saturday's game. But we couldn't do that with all the other kids there.

After we put the bucket of balls back in the trunk, I dropped Eric off at his house. Then Noah and I drove to my place. We went into the backyard and sat down on the bench. Noah pulled his knees up to his chest with his back up against one side like he often did. I leaned against the other side, looked at Noah, and said,

"I talked to your coach yesterday."

"You did? Why?"

"I felt like I owed him an apology."

"For what?"

"For yelling at him at the game."

Noah looked at me for a moment. Then he looked down and away.

"What?" I asked.

"So you think I was wrong, too? You think I should've lied about the catch?"

"Oh no." I said, "No, of course not. I needed to apologize because I yelled at him in public, in front of his team and in front of the crowd. You remember when we were playing workup, and Jayden said he caught the ball but he didn't?"

"Yeah."

"And remember why I told you that I didn't tell the truth about what I saw and call him a liar right then and there?"

"Because it would've made him feel bad in front of everyone."

"Right. Well, that's the problem with what I did on Saturday. I don't agree with Coach Tasker at all. I don't think he should have benched you. But I should've waited to talk to him in private. I was so mad that I yelled at him in front of everyone and embarrassed him. So I told him I was sorry. And he told me he wasn't mad at you and that you still had an even chance with Matt of playing second base."

"Really?"

"Yup."

"I just wanted to tell the truth."

"I know that."

"But it's kinda confusing."

"What do you mean?"

"Well, I wanted to do the Baseball Code, to tell the truth. But the code says 'always put the team first' too. And Coach Tasker says I let the team down."

"So what do you feel like you should have done?"

"I feel like I should've told the truth."

"Okay Noah. I think it's time for me to tell you the last part of the Baseball Code."

"There's more?"

"Yup. It's the very last part, and the most important. It says, 'Always do what's good, what's right.'"

"What does that mean?"

"It means you have to have balance; you have to look at the whole . . . um, let me think of a better way to explain it. You know what a sacrifice bunt is, right?"

"Yeah. It's when you bunt and get yourself out on purpose to get the runner on first to second base so he can score a run."

"Right. So if you look at the smaller piece, just the bunt itself, it looks like you made a bad play—like you did something wrong. But the point of the whole game is to get runs. So when you look at the whole, you did something important, something good."

"But what does that have to do with Coach Tasker benching me?"

"Well, Coach Tasker said he benched you because you didn't 'put the team first.' But 'putting the team first' is just one part of the code. You also have to "play fair' and 'tell the truth.' You can't put the team first by cheating. You have to look at the whole and balance everything."

"That seems hard."

"It can be. But here's the thing. When I asked you what you felt you should've done about your catch in the game, what did you say?"

"I said I felt like I should've told the truth."

"Right. You see, lots of times we already know what the balance is, what the good is. We just *feel* it. Remember when we were looking at baseball diamonds in your book? We talked about why baseball diamonds were beautiful, and we used math to describe it? We said the baseball diamond was like a—"

"Like a square."

"Right! And squares are beautiful because they're balanced. Every side is the same."

I pointed out at the garden.

"And we said it's the same with the roses. They're beautiful because they're balanced. All the petals are shaped the same, and they're all spaced equally around the center. But you don't have to know all that to know they're beautiful. You just *feel* their beauty.

"It's the same with what's good. You might be able to explain it. But you don't always have to. You can just *feel* it. In your heart, you sense the balance; you know what's good. So, what's the last part of the Baseball Code?"

"Always do what's good, what's right."

"That's it."

"And you think I did what was good, I mean, when I told the truth about the catch?"

"I sure do."

"But Coach Tasker doesn't."

"Well, I can tell you from experience that when it comes to telling the truth, the opinion you need to be the most concerned about is your own."

PART IX

LATE INNING SCARE

25

Eric's surgery went well. I visited him in the hospital along with Noah and his mom. Now he'd been discharged and was recuperating at home. Noah was going over regularly to spend time with him.

I got up early and went out back to put some water on the roses. When I was done, I sat down on the bench to rest for a few minutes. It was still cool with a light breeze. The air had that touch of sweet freshness in it. On the back side of the garden, a squirrel sat hunched on the brick border. He had picked up something in his tiny hands and was turning it over with curiosity. Beauty—that's what the garden always got me thinking about.

"I thought I'd find you here."

"What?"

I turned to see Noah standing behind me, his bat over his shoulder. I'd been so focused that I hadn't heard his footsteps. My hearing wasn't as sharp as it used to be.

"I knocked on the door. But when you didn't answer, I figured you'd be in the back."

"True enough."

"Are we walkin' or takin' your car?"

We were headed over to the field. It was Thursday. Tonight was Noah's last team practice before Coach Tasker made his decision about who got to play second base for the rest of the season. So Noah wanted to make sure he was ready.

"My glove and the bucket of balls are already in the trunk. Let's just drive."

We jumped in the car. I backed out and headed down the street. When we got to the field, no one else was there. So we started warming up.

"I was hoping we could work on double plays today," Noah said.

"Double plays? I can't imagine there are a lot of double plays in Summer League."

"I know. But Coach Tasker has us practice them, and I'm not that good at it."

"Well—"

"But it doesn't matter anyway since the other kids didn't come."

"I'm not so sure about that."

"But it's just you and me. That's not enough."

"Well, we'll have to be creative. Grab the bucket of balls and come out to second base."

"Okay, Coach."

Noah picked up the bucket, and we walked out to second.

"When you're playing second base, the hard part of a double play is catching the throw from the shortstop or third baseman, stepping on second, and then throwing the ball on to first. It's all one motion, and it happens fast."

"Okay. But we don't have enough players for a first baseman and a shortstop and someone to hit the ball."

"We don't need 'em. We don't need the first baseman just like we didn't need a catcher for batting practice, because we've got a whole bucket of baseballs. You just throw the ball to first.

When we run out of baseballs, we'll go pick 'em all up. We don't need someone to hit the ball because all you care about is catching the throw from the shortstop—not how he gets the ball.

"So I'll be the shortstop. I'll yell 'Hit' to signal the ball is hit. You'll run to get your foot on the bag. I'll throw the ball to you, you'll catch it, get off the bag, and fire to first. That way you'll practice the important parts of making a double play. Got it?"

"I think so."

I took the bucket of balls and walked over to shortstop. Noah got into position at second base. I picked a ball out of the bucket and yelled "Hit." Noah ran over and stood with one foot on second base as I threw him the ball. He caught it, turned, and threw the ball toward first.

"Okay," I said, "let's try something a little different."

I motioned to Noah to walk over to second base with me.

"Look," I said, "you did a great job of getting to second fast and getting your left foot on the back of the bag. But then you stopped and waited for the ball. You don't want to stop. You want to keep the motion going.

"You hit the bag with your left foot. You're looking for the throw." I demonstrated the motions as I talked. "When you see the ball coming, you step toward it with your right foot. As soon as it hits your mitt, you pull your left foot off the bag, step toward first base, and throw. It's almost a single motion. Remember what we said about the baseball diamond and the rose?"

"That they were beautiful?"

"Right. But their beauty comes from their symmetry—how the bases are all ninety feet apart and the rose petals are equally spaced around the center. The beauty here is different. It's in the motion.

"It's like the beauty of catching a fly ball. You time your running so that you stick out your arm just at the moment the ball falls out of the sky right into your glove. In a double play, you step on the bag, step toward the throw, catch it, step toward first, and fire the ball—all in one smooth motion. So let's get back to work."

"Okay."

Noah and I got back into position. I'd yell "Hit" and throw the ball. Sometimes Noah would get his feet tangled up and be off balance for the throw to first. Sometimes he fell back into his old habit of standing there and waiting for the ball. Sometimes my throws were so far off that we couldn't make a play at all. But we kept going. When the bucket was empty, we picked up the balls and started again, over and over.

It was beginning to get hot, and I was beginning to get tired. Noah was like I was as a kid. As long as there was someone willing to play, he was ready. He was tireless. But I wasn't. Just as I was about to call it quits, it started to click. I could tell Noah was feeling it. Then everything fell together.

I yelled "Hit." I waited a few seconds. Then I threw the ball. I watched Noah flow toward second base in what seemed like slow motion. His left foot stepped on the bag as his right foot stretched toward my throw. The ball popped into his mitt just as his foot hit the ground so that he pivoted his left foot off the bag, stepped toward first, and threw. One smooth, perfect, purposeful motion.

Noah looked over at me. We both smiled.

Beautiful.

After Noah and I climbed back into the car, I asked how Eric was doing. Noah said he was doing okay, but he missed getting outside, especially playing baseball. Then he added,

"Coach, I was thinking about giving Eric something."

"That's a nice thought."

"I mean, he's stuck in his house all the time. It's kinda boring. I was thinking about giving him something about baseball."

"That's great."

"But I wanted to ask you first."

"You mean about ideas for what to get?"

"No. I have an idea."

"What is it?"

"I wanted to give him the book you gave me—the one with the baseball fields."

But it was a gift—something I wanted you to have.

"So what do you think?" Noah asked.

"Why would you want to do that?"

"Remember when you gave me the book? You told me how beautiful you thought the baseball diamonds were, with the perfectly even dirt base paths with the white bases at the corners, and the green grass in the outfield?"

"Yeah."

"Well, I thought so too. And when I look at the book in my bed at night, I feel like I'm there, playing baseball in those beautiful places. It's like a dream, and it makes me feel good. So I thought since Eric can't go outside that maybe the book would help him feel like he was playing too, like it does for me."

I looked at Noah. What seemed intuitive to him as a way to help his friend only slowly broke through my resistance. Noah didn't want to give his book to Eric because he didn't care about it but *because* he cared about it, because it meant something to him. He didn't want to go and buy some random trinket at the store. He wanted to share something with his friend that his experience had told him was valuable. He was passing on our connection. He was keeping the garden blooming.

"Of course," I said, "that's perfect."

Instead of driving home with Noah and letting him walk

back to his house, I dropped him off first. Noah's idea had reminded me of something I needed to do.

～

When I got home, I went straight to the bedroom and took the box down from the shelf in the closet. My trophies were there on top. There was 'Most Improved Player' from the Apalachin Little League. I hadn't thought about those days for ages, about Bobby and Scott and five-hundred in our backyard.

Then there was the baseball team trophy from my senior year for first place in the Olympic League. We only lost two games that year. It was a magical season. I felt such cama-raderie with my teammates at a school that I hated when I first went there.

I pulled the trophies out of the box. Lying below was what I was looking for. It was the program from the first major league game I ever saw, the Dodgers/Mets game that my dad and I had gone to in 1962. On the front of it was a signature—Sandy Koufax.

Koufax hadn't signed it that night. It would've been impos-sible for us to get anywhere near him, and the seats we had weren't that close to the field. But years after, I got his signature at a special event. Then I put the program in a frame, and it hung on one wall or another for quite a few years.

It was a good conversation piece when I was young. But over time, other pictures became more fitting to the decor. So it found its resting place here. Of course, I knew where it was. I knew I could pull it out if there were occasion.

What Noah had reminded me of today was that it was the memory that mattered to me, not the memento, not the faded piece of paper, signed by a person I didn't know and never would. That memory wasn't going anywhere. But like Noah had done with his gift, I could use the memento to build yet more memories.

I took the program out of the frame and put it on the kitchen counter. Then I sat down in my chair, turned on Bach's Unaccompanied Cello Suites with Yo-Yo Ma, and picked up my book to do some reading.

26

I'd just got done putting the bench together. Susan and I had seen it at a store a couple of weeks earlier. We'd planted the last bush in the rose garden, and the bench seemed like the perfect finishing touch. It came in a box, and you had to put the legs on with bolts. The holes didn't line up perfectly, so it took longer than I thought it would.

After I broke the box down, I set it in the garage and put my tools back on the work bench. Then I went inside to wash my hands.

"Hey Susan. C'mon out and see the bench."

"Okay. Just a minute."

I dried my hands, went back outside, and sat down on the bench to wait. One of the reasons Susan liked roses so much was that she grew up around them. Her mom liked gardening, and they had a big flower garden in their backyard. It was kind of like me and baseball. My dad liked baseball. So I suppose that had rubbed off on me. But because of Susan, I had grown to appreciate roses too—their similarity of shape but unending variety of color.

Susan came out and sat down. There we were, sitting on the new bench for the first time, looking out across the garden. The sun was just setting. The air was warm and sweet. Then like she so often did, Susan just hit me with it out of nowhere.

"Who's your best friend?"

Susan was the only one who could get away with these kinds of questions. With most people, I'd simply refuse to answer. But Susan could draw me out because I loved talking with her. I always had. Her conversation was like a good game of catch. I never got tired of it.

That's what had drawn us closer together in the first place. She was thoughtful, but about practical matters, reflective without spinning off into theoretical flights of fancy that no one cared anything about.

"I guess I'd have to say Steve. I know I don't keep up with him as much as I ought to. But we've known each other since high school. That's about as long as I've known anyone."

"So I'm not your best friend?"

"C'mon, you tricked me."

"No I didn't. I asked you who your best friend was, and you said it was Steve."

"Yeah. But you know what I meant. When someone says 'best friend,' they're usually not talking about husband or wife. It's usually your best girl or guy friend. Of course, you're my best friend. But that's different. It doesn't count."

"Why shouldn't it count. You're *my* best friend."

"Oh, c'mon. Now you're just trying to make me feel bad."

Susan tossed her shoulders back and laughed her patented laugh.

"No I'm not," she said, "but I *am* trying to make a point. Husbands and wives should see each other as friends. Friendship is a big part of love, maybe even the biggest part."

"It's funny that you say that. My dad said something like that to me once when I was a kid."

"Really? That's interesting. I don't think my mom and dad were very good friends. I think maybe that's why they didn't stay together. You know, Aristotle thought that having friends was one of the most important parts of life. He said that nobody would choose to live without friends even if they had everything else."

"That sounds like something from one of the lit classes you took back in college."

"Nope. It's from the Intro to Philosophy class I took as a breadth requirement. The Greeks even had a special word for the love between friends."

A piece of paper had blown into the garden and was resting against the bottom of one of the roses. I stood up, walked over and picked it up. Then I sat back down up against the side of the bench so I could turn toward Susan.

"So if it's so important, how do you think you become friends with someone?" I asked.

"By spending time together. By talking with each other and getting to know what's important to each other."

"But if it takes time, you're not going to become friends with everyone. So how do you choose? Why do you become friends with some people and not others?"

Susan looked out across the garden for a few moments. It reminded me again of how a good conversation was so much like a good game of catch. A harder question was like a tough ground ball thrown to your right. You had to take a step or two, reach across your body, and backhand it. It took a little more time to get it, straighten up, and throw it back.

Susan looked back at me.

"Well, sometimes it's just happenstance, like with kids. When you're young, you might be friends with the kid next door just because she's the kid next door. My best friend growing up lived across the street from me. Even with adults, maybe someone is your co-worker or your next-door neighbor.

But at other times, the reason is you have something in common. There could be a lot of kids in your class at school. But one of them likes baseball like you do or one of them likes math."

"That makes sense, but I've had friends I didn't have a lot in common with too. Steve is a good example."

I could tell that now Susan was really getting interested. Her eyes were opened wide, and she was leaning forward.

"Right—of course—because having a common interest or living next door is just the occasion, the starting point. So it could be something else entirely, like a chance meeting or someone asking you for help. For men and women it's often sexual attraction. The guy thinks she's pretty, or she thinks he's handsome. But whether it's proximity, or common interest, or romance, all of that is only a hook, something that draws people together to get the process started."

"What process?"

"The process of building friendship, spending time together, getting to know what's important to each other, learning to care for each other."

"Okay, it makes sense to me that friendships start in different ways, but romantic relationships just seem different."

"In what way?" Susan asked.

"Well, I wouldn't want to reduce a romantic relationship to just a friendship. I mean, what I feel for you isn't the same as what I feel for my other friends."

"But that's the point. It's not reducing. It's adding. A romantic relationship starts in a different way. The feelings are different, and they might even stay that way. But if it doesn't also develop into a friendship, then it isn't likely to survive."

"You think it's that essential?"

"Yes. What I'm saying is that friendship is the heart of all relationships. Interests may change, romance may wax and wane, but friendship is what endures. It's like the roses. They look good when we plant them. But they only stay healthy because we take the time to water them, pull the weeds, and replenish the soil. They only stay healthy because we put in the work. That's what building friendship does for relationships. Friendship keeps the garden growing."

27

I pulled into the lot at the park around 6:15 p.m. Normally, I didn't go to team practices, but I was determined to watch Noah's last practice before Coach Tasker made his decision. I didn't know how good Matt was. But if Noah played anything like he had at our field this morning, I was sure he would be hard to beat.

After I locked the car, I walked over to the diamond. I climbed up into the stands right away and found a seat near the top. I didn't want to wait around down below and try to talk to Noah. First, I didn't want to make him nervous by letting him know I was watching him. But second, I had no interest in running into Coach Tasker. Our conversation at the diner went better than I had expected, but I wasn't going to push my luck.

Noah wasn't out on the field yet. The practice didn't officially start until 6:30 p.m., so that wasn't surprising. Matt was there warming up with another kid that I didn't know. Coach Tasker was fiddling around with some equipment in the bench area.

Maybe I had misjudged him. After all, aside from the one incident with the missed call, he had been reasonable. What he told me was true—he had put in a lot of work with the kids. And Noah seemed to like him okay. Still I didn't like him benching Noah for telling the truth. So the jury was still out with me.

It was a typical warm, California summer evening. Watching the kids running around throwing the ball made me feel good at a visceral level. It took me back. I remembered my own days in Little League, how great it was playing on a real field for the first time.

Nothing was as important to me as baseball in those days, and nothing was more fun. I played ball with my friends during the day, fell asleep listening to the Dodgers' game, and dreamed about baseball all night.

I looked around the field again. Practice was starting up and still no Noah. This was strange. Noah had worked so hard, and now it was down to the wire. This practice could make the difference. Maybe I should give Ashley a call. But that would be strange too.

Then the phone in my pocket buzzed. I fumbled for it, and pulled it out. It was Ashley.

"Hello."

"Hi Terry." Her voice was shaky. "Terry . . ."

"Yes."

"Terry, it's Eric. Something went wrong. He's in the hospital. Noah and I are here too. Can you come, I mean, Noah wants you to come."

"I'll be right there."

I ran to my car. My heart was pounding, and my mind was spinning scenarios. I couldn't imagine what had happened. He was doing fine, and he was so young.

The hospital was only a couple of miles away. I drove as fast as I could. I was there in less than five minutes and went in through the emergency entrance. Ashley and Noah were sitting in the waiting area.

"What happened? How's Eric?"

"We don't know," Ashley said. "Noah was over at his house, and Eric starting having pain in his leg. Then it got really bad. His mom called 911, and they sent an ambulance. We followed them over. His mom is in there with him now."

Noah looked scared. He was cuddled up to his mom. She had her arm around him. I sat down on his other side.

"I'm sure he'll be okay, buddy," I said, squeezing Noah's knee.

"I hope so. Eric was crying. It was pretty scary."

Just then, Eric's mom came out of the emergency room area and walked toward us.

"They're taking him into surgery. The doctor said it's a blood clot. It sometimes happens, particularly after surgery on a leg like this. But they caught it before it moved, and they're going to remove it."

A blood what? I didn't hear the words fully. It was like garbled speech. My mind refused to process the sounds.

"Did they say how long it would be," Ashley asked?

"No. They didn't really give me any idea."

"Well, sit down here. We're going to wait with you. Can I get you a cup of coffee?" Ashley asked.

"No thanks. I'm not sure I'm up for hospital coffee at the moment. Look, I appreciate your waiting with me. But I know from what Noah and Eric were talking about earlier that Noah has an important baseball practice tonight. He should go ahead and go. There's nothing he can do by sitting around here."

"That's true, Noah," Ashley said. "We're all just going to sit here and wait. So maybe you should go to your practice."

"No, Mom. I don't wanna go. I don't care what happens or what Coach Tasker thinks. Eric is my friend. I just feel like I should be here."

I jumped in.

"Why don't I run over to the park and let Coach Tasker know what's going on. Then I can stop on my way back and get some good coffee for everyone. How's that sound?"

I pushed through both doors and into the parking lot. I did want to help Noah with Coach Tasker, but mostly, I had to get out of there. I needed to get my body moving to keep my mind from slipping away.

I raced down the road to the park. I jumped out of the car and walked as fast as I could without breaking into a run until I got to the diamond. Coach Tasker was out on the field, hitting ground balls to the kids. I paced up and down along the chain link fence, trying to attract his attention. Finally, he saw me and walked over.

"You look like a caged tiger over here, Terry. What's troublin' you?"

"Hi Bob," I said. "I wanted to let you know why Noah isn't at practice tonight."

"Okay. What's brewin'?"

"His best friend was rushed to the emergency room and has been taken into emergency surgery."

"Well, I'm real sorry to hear that. That's terrible. Please tell Noah that I'll have the whole team say a prayer for his friend at the end of practice tonight."

"Thank you. I just wanted to let you know. I knew this was an important practice since it was the last one before your decision."

"Oh, that. Nah. I already made up my mind on that before tonight."

"You did? What did you decide?"

"Well, now, I can't tell you before I tell the boys. That wouldn't be kosher, would it? I'll be lettin' 'em know before the game on Saturday. Now be sure to tell Noah how sorry I am about his friend."

"I will. Thanks."

I got back in the car, but I didn't hit the starter. I leaned back in the seat and stared out through the windshield.

"It was a blood clot," the doctor said.

He was standing there in his green scrubs.

"It was a blood clot. There was nothing we could do. I'm very sorry."

"But she was fine. She was perfectly healthy. That's not possible—"

"Blood clots are unpredictable. It moved to her lung. There was nothing we could do."

I stood up when I saw him coming into the room. He was standing there in his green scrubs. I could see his lips moving. I was starting to shake.

"I'm very sorry," he said. "There was nothing—"

"But—"

"There was nothing—"

I had to do something to pull myself back. I slammed my palms against the steering wheel, over and over, until I couldn't think anymore, I could only feel the pain and pressure in my hands. Then I took a deep breath and started the car.

I drove to the coffee kiosk and ordered three coffees and some cream to go, and a bottle of juice for Noah. Then I headed back to the hospital. When I got there, I didn't pull right into the parking lot. I circled the block a few times. It seemed like something in my very muscles was holding me back.

I knew I had to get inside before the coffee cooled down. So I turned into the lot, parked, and walked into the waiting area. I passed out the coffee and juice. There hadn't been any further update about Eric. I sat down beside Noah and told him what Coach Tasker had said.

We all waited. Sometimes we talked. Sometimes we got up and walked around. Mostly we sat in silence. One thing I had learned through the years was the importance of just being present. It wasn't so important what you said, but that you were there. We were all there. And we waited together.

After several hours, the doctor appeared in his green scrubs, standing in front of us.

"Eric is doing well," he said. "We caught the clot early, and we were able to break it up and remove it surgically. He's going to be fine."

PART X

BOTTOM OF THE NINTH

28

Friday came and went. Eric was recovering well in the hospital. On Saturday morning, I stopped by the post office on my way to see Pastor Thompson. I walked over to the supply counter and picked up a priority mail envelope. I put the program signed by Koufax inside along with the brief note I had written to my friend who had agreed to send me three of his company's season tickets for another Dodger game. Then I sealed it up and addressed it.

I got in line. When it was my turn, I handed the envelope to the clerk. He put the postage sticker on and ran through the routine questions about whether there was anything dangerous inside and so forth. When he was done, I asked,

"How long will it take to get there?"

"Well, priority packages are one to three days. But I'd give it four to five to be sure."

This time I was prepared. I wasn't going silently again.

"If it's one to three days for priority mail, then why do I need to give it four to five?"

"Oh, yeah. Sure, it's one to three days, especially since you're just sending it across the city. That should be fine."

"Okay—"

"But you never know."

"Never know about what?"

"About whether it might take another day or two."

"But you just said one to three days especially since it's close."

"Yeah, of course. I'm sure there won't be a problem. I wouldn't worry about it. One to three days."

"Okay. Thanks."

I started to walk away.

"But I'd give it a couple days extra."

I turned my head back.

"What?"

"You know, just to be sure."

I knew when I was beaten.

Pastor Thompson was expecting me this time. I'd called ahead and made an appointment. He saw me coming through the window and waved me in.

"Hey TR, good to see you."

He stood up and stuck his hand out across the desk. I clasped his hand and gave it a firm shake.

"Hi John. Thanks for seeing me."

"Have a seat, TR. I was sorry to hear about Eric. Ashley called me afterwards. I understand you were at the hospital. I guess he's doing okay."

"Yeah. The doctor says he should be fine. It was a bit of a scare though."

"Is that what brings you here?"

"No. Not really, although it did bring up some difficult memories."

"I can imagine. How are you doing with all that?"

"Sometimes better than others. But I think I'm on the right path."

"Okay. But remember what I said. I'm always here if you need to talk. And it couldn't hurt you to get back into the small group meetings."

"I know. Thanks. I appreciate it."

"So what did you want to talk about?"

"I guess I just wanted to bounce something off you, an idea I had."

"Okay. Shoot."

Pastor Thompson put his hands behind his head and leaned back in his chair.

"Do you remember when we talked last time, I mentioned the verse from Job where 'the morning stars sang together, and all the heavenly beings shouted for joy'? I said it made me think about a deep joy woven into the fabric of the universe that can't be reached by our understanding."

"Yeah. I remember you said it was helpful to you."

"Right. Well, I think I know what it might be—the deep joy woven into the fabric of the universe."

Pastor Thompson smiled.

"That's interesting."

"You remember that I've been helping Noah with baseball and math?"

"Yup."

"Well, Noah and I have been working in my garden a little too. And we've talked about the beauty of baseball and the beauty of the roses. I told him how mathematics can describe that beauty by describing symmetry, the shape of the ball diamond and the curve of the rose petals. Then we talked about how mathematics also describes what's true—"

Pastor Thompson interrupted me.

"It sounds like you're working on a sermon."

"Hardly. But what I was thinking was that if what is beautiful is often true, and if what is true is often right and good, then maybe they're all really the same thing in different forms, I mean, beauty, truth, and goodness. So I asked myself what ties them together, what lies at the core?"

Pastor Thompson leaned forward with his hands together and his elbows on the desk.

"Do you have an answer or are you gonna leave me hangin'?"

"Well, Susan used to say that love was more about action than feeling. It was about doing good in the world. So it got me thinking that goodness was just love in action."

"I'm following."

"But I also noticed that when we see someone do something really good for someone else, we're often tempted to say, 'That's beautiful.' It's like when we feel the love that someone has put into action, it feels like beauty to us.

"So then I wondered if all beauty, like roses and sunsets, weren't just our feeling the love at the root of all things, our feeling the love of it all. I mean, doesn't the Bible say love is the 'greatest of all'?"

"True," Pastor Thompson replied.

"And that's the final piece," I said. "Truth. It didn't seem to fit for a while, and then it hit me. Susan said the Greeks had a special word for the love between friends. I looked it up, and it's the same word that's in 'philosophy'—the love of wisdom, the desire to know the truth."

Pastor Thompson looked at me for a moment. Then he said, "I thought you told me you were a mathematician, not a theologian."

I smiled.

"Well, after all, it is another kind of Theory of Everything—

it's love. Love is the deep joy woven into the fabric of the universe. It's the core that ties everything together. When we act it out, we call it goodness. When we think about it, we call it truth. When we feel it, we call it beauty."

29

The ball popped into my glove. I loved that sound. I swung my arm around and opened it, releasing the ball into the air. Then I grabbed it with my bare hand and fired it back to my dad.

"Now don't go showboatin'," he said.

"I'm just foolin' around."

He threw it back high and I reached up to grab it.

"Hey, Dad?"

"Yeah."

"Do you think I'll ever get married?"

"Wow. That came outta left field. Why do you ask?"

"I don't know. How old were you when you got married to Mom?"

"I was twenty-one, and your mom was twenty."

"Did you know each other for a long time?"

"Yeah. We grew up together in the same small town. We had known each other since we were in grade school."

I missed a ball my dad threw low and had to turn around and chase it down. When I got back to my spot, I tossed it back and said,

"That's amazing. I don't have any friends that I've known that long."

"Well, that's because we've moved around, and you've changed schools. First, we moved from New York to California. Then when your first school here closed down, you changed to the one you go to now. But in the small town where I grew up, everyone pretty much stayed put."

"So how did you know you wanted to marry Mom?"

Dad caught my throw, took the ball out of his glove, and held it in his right hand.

"Is there something you're not telling me? You're not planning on getting married on me are you?"

"Daad! I'm only in the ninth grade!"

Dad laughed and tossed the ball high up in the air so that I had to wait for it to come down.

"Well, why all the questions? Is there a girl you like?"

"Yeah, probably, I mean, I don't know."

"What do you mean you don't know? Do you like someone or not?"

It was my turn to catch the ball and hold on to it.

"I'm not throwin' it back if you're gonna hassle me."

"I'm not hassling you. You brought it up. I'm just asking. Is there a girl you like?"

"Yeah, I guess so."

"Does she like you?"

"I don't know. I don't really talk to her. I'm kinda shy around girls."

"That's okay. We could use more of that these days. Here comes a grounder."

Dad threw one on the ground to my right. I had to take a quick step and backhand it.

"Good snag!" Dad said.

"Thanks. But you never answered my question."

"What was that?"

"How did you know you wanted to marry Mom? How do you know when you're in love?"

"Do you think you're in love?"

"I don't know. Maybe sometimes I feel like I might be."

My dad caught the ball. Then he took off his glove with the ball in it and stuck it under his arm.

"Let's sit down for a minute," he said.

We walked over to the patio and sat down on the picnic table bench.

"Look," Dad said, "Feelings between boys and girls is a tough one. You might have romantic feelings for a girl because she smiles at you, or because she's pretty, or because someone told you she likes you. And romantic feelings are nice things, but they aren't the same thing as love."

"Then how do you know the difference? How do you know when you're in love?"

"I have to be honest and tell you that I don't know for sure. But there is one thing that I do know. You can't be in love with a girl if you aren't good friends with her first. Real love follows friendship, not the other way around."

"But what if I'm too shy to talk to her? How do I become friends?"

"That's a good question. And it's something you're going to have to work on. But your mom will probably be better at helping you with that than I will be. I was a little like you when I was your age—shy around girls."

"Really?"

"Yup."

"How did you get over it?"

"I guess I got older." Dad smiled. "And I met the right girl."

"How do you know when you meet the right girl?"

"It's the one that you want to be your best friend."

~

It was late summer, almost fall, and still plenty warm in L.A. I was already certain about Susan. I'd never met anyone like her. She was beautiful, smart, brimming with interests and energy. I was going to ask her tonight. I wasn't sure exactly how. But I knew exactly where. It had to be at Zuma beach, where we had our first conversation about love.

We had dinner, a little late. Then we hopped in my VW Bug and drove over Malibu Canyon at dusk. It was a clear night. The moon was bright, and the mountains were silhouetted cutouts against the dimming sky. The ride was beautiful. We rolled the windows down and let the breeze blow across our faces.

I wanted to remember everything about that drive—the curves of the mountain road, the smell of the air, the ease of Susan's smile, the feeling of freedom and future. I wanted to breathe it in and record it, to not let a moment of it escape.

When we got to Zuma, we took off our shoes and left them in the car before we locked it up and walked down to the water's edge. We wanted to feel the sand and water on our feet. We held hands and walked along the shore.

"Do you remember the first time we came here together?" I asked.

"Yes. You splashed water on me."

"You're the one who started that."

"Probably. That sounds like me."

"And if I remember correctly, you got caught in a rip current."

"And you rescued me."

"Well, I'd like to think so. But I don't remember your being in much real danger."

"I don't know. I probably got out a little far."

"And I got in a little over my head."

Susan stopped walking and turned and looked at me.

"What does that mean?"

I chuckled. "It doesn't mean anything. It means I didn't really know you very well back then, and you started talking about the nature of love, and I knew I liked you, and it made me nervous. I didn't know how to react."

We started walking again.

"That's funny," Susan said. "I never thought anything about it."

"That's because you were always confident. I was more uncertain of myself, and I wanted you to like me."

"You always seemed plenty confident to me."

I smiled.

"I can put on a good act when I put my mind to it. Anyway, being arrogant isn't really the same thing as being confident."

I had no idea what I was doing. I had meant to ask her as soon as we got down to the water. But I was too nervous. Now that I missed the moment, I wasn't sure how to circle back.

"We should probably turn around," Susan said.

"Yeah." We turned and started walking back.

"Do you still feel the same way about love?" I asked.

"In what sense?"

"That love is an action rather than a feeling."

"I don't think I would say it's either—or. There's obviously feeling involved. But feelings can come and go. So I think there needs to be something deeper too, something that involves action and commitment."

"So how do you feel now?"

I knew it was stupid as soon as I said it. Where was I going with this?

"About what?" Susan asked.

"About us?"

Susan stopped again and looked at me.

"Terry?"

"Yeah."

"What are you trying so hard not to say?"

I took both of her hands. My heart was pounding through my chest. I was at a complete loss for words. I just blurted it out.

"Will you marry me?"

Susan tossed her shoulders back and around and laughed. The freckles across her nose sparkled in the moonlight.

"Is that why we came here tonight? Is that what you've been trying to ask? Yes, of course, who else would I marry?"

She pulled me close and kissed me. Then she wrapped her arms around me and held me tight. We stood there for what seemed forever with her head on my shoulder, her soft brown hair against my face, and the cool salt water washing over our feet and taking all my uncertainty with it.

It was in that moment that I knew that love was something beyond, that it was more, that it was mystical. It included romance, but it neither started nor stopped there. It flowed through romance and then on to everything else that it touched.

30

Saturday afternoon, I drove to the park for Noah's game. Ashley had taken him over earlier. She was already sitting in the stands. I climbed up the bleachers and sat down next to her.

"Hi Ashley. How's it going," I asked.

As she was about to respond, her phone rang.

"Just a moment," she said.

She reached into her purse and pulled out the phone. I turned my attention to the field. The kids were warming up, playing catch in groups of two or three. I picked out Noah. This was the day he'd been waiting for, the day he found out Coach Tasker's choice. He looked pretty relaxed. But it was hard to tell from this distance.

"Terry."

Ashley's voice grabbed my attention back.

"Yeah."

"Hey, I'm sorry to ask you this at the last minute, really. But can you take Noah home after the game. That was work on the phone. I have to go in. I'm really sorry."

"Of course, no problem. I'm here for the duration anyway. I'm sorry you can't stay, but I'll get him home."

"Thanks, Terry. I appreciate it."

With that, she stepped down the bleachers and headed toward the parking lot. I felt bad for Ashley that she wasn't going to get to watch Noah play. But I wasn't unhappy to be left alone. I liked Ashley. But she tended to talk during the games. I preferred to watch the play and not be distracted.

I turned my attention back toward the field. Coach Tasker had just waved the kids in to the bench area. The game was going to start in a few minutes. The kids had gathered around, and Tasker was talking to them. This was the moment. I was sure this was when Coach Tasker was telling them who was going to play second base for the rest of the season.

I couldn't help but think back to the ups and downs of my own Little League and high school experience. It was so distant now and in many ways seemed insignificant. But at the time it was the most important thing in the world. I lived and died with every win or loss, with every good or bad play, with every decision the coach made. I felt for Noah.

Noah's team was home team today, so they'd be taking the field when the game started. I was getting more nervous by the minute. The team was still gathered around the coach, listening. Then the huddle broke and they all ran out onto the field. I looked for Noah. I spotted him, and my heart sunk. He was standing in left field.

I quickly shifted my eyes to second base. There was Matt. How could this be? Noah was playing so well. There was no way he wasn't the best choice. I knew it! I knew Tasker wasn't to be trusted. All that down home friendly banter. It made it seem like there was nothing to worry about. I should've known. This was all because I yelled at him in public and told him he was wrong. It was because Noah missed the last practice to be with Eric.

I was fuming. I wanted to march right down to the field again and tell Tasker what I thought with no reservations. But I knew better. I couldn't do that to Noah. He had to live with the decision for the rest of the season no matter what. I'd already done enough.

I looked out at Noah standing in left field. He seemed strangely relaxed, like earlier during warm-ups. He didn't look angry or upset. His head was in the game. He was crouched down, rocking side to side in expectation, eyes fixed on the batter.

I remembered that I had told Noah that I would video some of the game. I thought I'd mostly do that when he was at bat, but I pulled the phone out of my pocket and focused it on Noah to see what it looked like from this distance. It was clear I needed to get closer.

I climbed down the rungs of the bleachers. Then I walked over toward the fence by left field. I didn't want to get so close that Noah would see me and be distracted. So I stopped in a group of parents that were standing there to watch the game. I focused my phone's camera on Noah and set it to 'video.' No sooner had I done that than I heard the crack of the bat. Noah started running back and to his right. I struggled to keep him in the frame.

Noah was running full speed as he neared the ball. He threw his left arm across his body, and leapt. You could see his outstretched arm high above his head. The ball smacked into his glove, and the glove closed around it. Noah came down, stopped, turned, and threw the ball as hard as he could back toward the infield.

The umpire threw his right fist into the air to signal a catch. Noah's teammates were jumping up and down. The crowd was on its feet cheering. I checked my video. I had caught the whole thing on my camera. I decided staying right where I was would be best for the rest of the game. I even had a clear view of home plate.

The top of the inning closed out with the opposing team

getting only one hit and no runs. When Noah came up in the bottom of the first, we had a runner on first and third with two outs. I focused my phone's camera on home plate. The pitcher was a big guy who was throwing hard. The first pitch to Noah was a fast ball down the middle. Noah swung hard, but he was behind it and missed. Strike one. The next one was high and away. Noah let it go.

He stepped out of the batter's box, took a couple of swings, and stepped back in. The next pitch was way inside. Noah jumped back. Concern rippled through the crowd, but Noah had gotten out of the way in time. It was two and one.

The pitcher threw again. It looked outside from my angle. Noah started to swing, then pulled back. But the umpire signaled strike. Noah looked over his shoulder at his coach. Then he focused back on the pitcher who threw one in the dirt. The catcher blocked it, and the runners stayed where they were. The count was full.

The next pitch looked like it was outside and a little high. But it was close. It might catch the outside corner. Noah swung and sent a foul ground ball down the first base sideline. The following one was a little low. Noah swung and tipped it into the ground and off the catcher's shin guard.

"Look at that," I said to myself. "He's guarding the plate. He's determined. He's not gonna go down looking." The next pitch was way outside, Noah was on with a walk, and the bases were loaded.

Unfortunately, the kid after Noah popped up to the pitcher, and the inning was over. Noah didn't get a lot more action in left field through the rest of the game—some routine fly balls and a few grounders, but nothing spectacular.

As far as hitting, Noah came up to bat in the third, his team's big inning, when they scored four of their five runs, but he grounded out. Then he struck out in the fourth. When he came up to the plate in the bottom of the sixth, they were behind six to five. There was a man on first and one out. Summer League only went for six innings. So this was it.

I focused the camera tight on home plate again. The first pitch was inside. Noah backed away. He stepped back in and squared up. The next pitch was down the middle. Noah lifted his back elbow, stepped forward, and swung. I heard the crack as the ball hit the sweet spot. It jumped off the bat and sailed into the gap between left and center. Both fielders took off running, but it was clear that they wouldn't get to it in time.

Noah took off toward first with the other runner speeding toward second in front of him. By the time Noah rounded second, one of the fielders had gotten to the ball, picked it up, and thrown it toward the shortstop who had run out to cut off the throw. It was certain now that the first runner was going to score. Noah hit third base and didn't even give the coach a glance. He had no intention of slowing down. He was going for home.

The shortstop had the ball. He turned and fired it toward home plate. It was a good throw. Noah was coming down the line. The ball bounced just before the plate, right toward the catcher's mitt, as Noah went into a slide.

It was all arms and legs and dust. I held my breath, and then I saw it—the ball rolling in the dirt. The umpire crossed his arms and threw them out to the side. Safe! Noah was safe, and he had scored the winning run!

Everyone in the stands was yelling and cheering. As soon as Noah stood up, his teammates ran out from the bench and mobbed him. The first ones who got there were trying to lift him up in the air. As the others piled on, they jumped up over the top, trying to touch his head or his shoulders. A bouncing mound of bodies began to form. Then it became unbalanced and tumbled to the ground—one wriggling mass of chaotic joy.

I hung back and drank it all in. It was the perfect baseball moment.

~

After the team was done celebrating and Coach Tasker had met with them for a few minutes to debrief, I found Noah to let him know that I'd be taking him home and that he could stay at my place until his mom got back from work. As we walked to the parking lot, Noah couldn't contain his excitement.

"Did you see that, Coach?"

"I sure did."

"That's the best hit I've had all season. And right when we needed it. I couldn't believe it!"

"It wasn't just the hit," I said. "You also showed some speed around the bases. And that was a nice slide into home."

"Yeah. But after the game, Coach Tasker said I should've looked at the third base coach. He might've stopped me at third since there was only one out, and I could've had a good chance of scoring from third later."

"Well, he's not entirely wrong about that," I said. "But as they say, 'All's well that ends well.' You scored, and that's all that matters now."

We climbed into the car.

"Seat belt on?" I asked.

"Yup."

I started the car, backed it out, and turned out onto the street.

"So what did Coach Tasker say about second base?"

Noah didn't respond right away.

"Is it something you don't want to talk about?"

"No. I do. But not here. Maybe when we get to your house."

"Okay . . . Boy, I can't get over it. A home run. You know, I think if there had been fences on the field, that would have been an over the fence homer. You really smacked it."

"Did you get a video of it?"

"Well, I got a shot when you hit it. And I got the play at

home plate. I couldn't follow the ball through the air. It was too small and moving too fast."

"That's still pretty good."

"Yeah it is."

We pulled into the garage.

"Can we go out back?" Noah asked.

"Sure."

We walked into the backyard and sat down on the bench by the rose garden. Noah leaned back against one side and pulled his knees up to his chest. I probably should have waited for him to say something. But my curiosity and frustration about the whole matter got the best of me.

"So what did Coach Tasker have to say about your playing second base? Did he explain why he decided to give the position to Matt instead?"

"He didn't give it to Matt."

"What?"

"He gave the position to me."

"But you were in left field today. Does it start next game or something?"

"No. I told him I didn't want it, that he should give the position to Matt."

"Why? I thought that's what you wanted. What you worked so hard for?"

"It is. But my dad called yesterday. He said that he couldn't come out this summer because of his job. He wanted me to go there to visit him instead. But if I go, I'll miss the last two weeks of the season."

"Okay."

"My mom said I don't have to go if I don't want to because I've worked hard to play on the team. But I want to see my dad."

"I get that. But I think Coach Tasker would understand and let you play second while you're here."

"Maybe. But Coach Tasker said that part of the decision was

who was most committed to the team. So I thought about the code, the Baseball Code—to put the team first and play fair. I *could* stay here and put the team first. But I'm the one who's choosing not to. So I think it's fair that Matt should get to play second."

"That's one way of looking at it," I said. "But it's a pretty big sacrifice on your part."

"I guess. But remember when you said that the Baseball Code wasn't just about baseball?"

"Yeah."

"And you said that you had to look at everything, at the whole, not just the pieces?"

"Yup."

"Well, if I just look at the baseball team and think about playing second base, then it seems like I'm giving something up, like maybe it's a bad idea—because I love baseball. But I love my dad more. So when I look at the whole thing, it doesn't seem like a bad idea. It seems like something good. It's like a sacrifice bunt."

I was speechless.

I looked out across the rose garden and I saw truth and goodness blooming everywhere. I looked back at Noah with his knees pulled up to his chest, his dark brown hair falling across his forehead, and the depth of insight behind his eyes. And I said the only thing I could think to say.

"That's beautiful."

EPILOGUE

The next few weeks went by quickly. I videoed Noah's last games. Then I used the software on my computer to put together a highlights reel for him to show his dad. We even included a few bloopers that Noah, Eric, and I watched over and over and laughed at till our sides hurt.

Eric was healing well. He was up and walking. The doctor said the initial surgery had been a success and that he might walk normally again and even run. The electronic tickets I had been waiting for from my friend arrived on my phone. So Noah, Eric, and I all went to a Dodger game together.

We ate hot dogs, peanuts, and ice cream. Noah and Eric cheered and yelled and mixed up the words to "Take Me Out to the Ball Game." They could barely stay in their seats. They were chattering and laughing and poking each other. At times, I think they forgot I was there at all. But I couldn't have cared less. They had the time of their lives.

Finally, the day arrived for Noah's departure to visit his father. I was sitting in my chair, looking at the Renoir print on the wall and waiting for a knock on the door. I knew Noah would be coming to say goodbye.

I was thinking about that knock on the door a few months earlier when I first saw Noah standing beside his mom in his jeans and Jurassic Park T-shirt. Nothing that day had prepared me for what was to come—for catch, for the field, for the Dodger game, for Eric, for Summer League, for the Baseball Code.

I knew the Code was just a cipher, a way for Noah to summon the strength and insight that was always there inside him, a way to talk about the journey we were on together. I also knew it was time to tell Noah some truth of my own. So when he knocked on the door, I opened it and said,

"Hey Noah. Come in. I'd like you to help me with something."

"Okay, Coach. What is it?"

"C'mon, I'll show you."

We walked through the house into the garage where I picked up a couple pairs of gardening gloves and pruning shears and handed some to Noah. Then we walked out into the backyard and over to the rose bed. I slipped gloves on my hands. I placed my left hand lightly around the stem of a rose and cut it about eighteen inches below the flower. I placed it on the grass beside the bed.

"Do it like that, but watch out for the thorns. Even with gloves they can poke you. We want to cut about a dozen or so. The ones that are in full bloom."

"Okay."

Noah started working beside me. He had become a fast learner. He cut a rose and mimicked my motion as he laid it gently beside mine on the grass.

"What are they for? Do you have a girlfriend or something?"

"Kind of. You'll see."

When we were almost finished, I said,

"Go cut one off the new rose bush we planted in the center."

Noah walked to the center of the garden, bent down and cut a deep red bloom from the bush. He walked back and placed it on top of the others.

"Okay, that's it," I said.

I picked up the roses and headed back to the garage with Noah following me.

"Just put your gloves and pruning shears on the bench there."

I cut a piece of twine, tied it around the stems, and then put the roses on the back seat of the car.

"Hop in," I said.

"Where are we going?"

"Not far. We'll be right back."

Noah hopped in. I got behind the wheel, started the car, and backed out. We drove in silence about a quarter mile. Then I pulled over to the curb alongside the trim green grass of a cemetery.

"Is this where we're going?" Noah asked.

"Yup. Grab the roses and come with me."

We walked about fifty yards across the grass and stopped beside a pink granite grave marker. On one side, were engraved the words, "In Loving Memory, Susan Anne Richards." The other side was engraved with a beautiful rose plant.

Noah stood and looked at the marker for a few moments. Then he asked,

"Was she your wife?"

"Yes."

Noah pointed at the date on the marker.

"Is that when she died?"

"Yes. It was a year ago last spring."

I took the roses from Noah and placed them on the ground in front of the marker.

"Is that why the rose bush was so special?"

"Yes. The rose garden was for her."

"Do you think you'll see her again, I mean, in heaven?"

"Yeah. But I miss her now every day because I still love her a lot."

We stood there together side by side without talking until Noah broke the silence.

"Well, then I love her too."

"That's good," I said, putting my arm across his shoulders, "because there's plenty of love to go around."

That's what Susan always said.

ACKNOWLEDGMENTS

I want to thank my brother, Ken, whose own fascinating novels helped to encourage me to try my hand at it as well. He also read an early version of *The Baseball Code* and offered several useful suggestions. My good friend, Thompson Brandt, read a number of drafts, caught many errors, gave invaluable advice, and had many lengthy conversations with me about both content and style. I cannot thank him enough. My son, Aaron, assisted me with some technical aspects of the cover design and also helped me gain more clarity in various passages. Finally, I owe my deepest gratitude to my wife, Myra, who was the first to read the manuscript, chapter by chapter as it emerged. She not only offered sage advice at every turn and painstakingly proofed every draft, but inspired me both to begin and to continue with her positive and loving encouragement.

Made in United States
Orlando, FL
09 July 2025

62783882R00146